THE
flower
WORKSHOP

Lessons in arranging blooms, branches,
fruits, and foraged materials

Ariella Chezar with Julie Michaels

Photography by Erin Kunkel

TEN SPEED PRESS
Berkeley

to my family

contents

•

Introduction

Is there anything that can transform a moment, a morning, a mood, or a space as instantly as an array of fresh flowers? Their color and aliveness, their fragrance, their movement, their ability to attract the eye (and distract it!), and the sheer sensual pleasure they give make them nearly miraculous.

While some of my favorite varieties, combinations, and ingredients have changed since I started my company almost twenty years ago, my design philosophy and devotion to color, texture, and seasonality are as vital to me as ever.

Over the years, I've been asked to share my floral philosophy in a variety of workshop settings. I've held these classes on flower farms in California and the Netherlands, at Hawaiian resorts, and in New York, Charleston, and other major cities. Depending on the location, I'll take my students foraging in the woods or roaming the aisles of a local flower market. We'll then spend time prepping each blossom; studying color, containers, and placement; and fashioning arrangements and bouquets that reflect not only my design philosophy but my deep love of flowers. My aim, to quote poet Mary Oliver, is to work until "I can hear the almost unhearable sound of the roses singing."

This book is meant to inspire. The following chapters show how to make arrangements that light up a dinner, spark a party, or decorate a wedding. Step-by-step instructions are included for every arrangement, but don't feel limited to the flowers I've selected. I'd prefer that you adopt my philosophy of floral design and use these recipes as a starting point. If you understand the concept of tone-on-tone arranging, of using a variety of blooms in similar colors, and if you learn to forage in your backyard and let what you find spark your creativity, you will come away with a point of view that can be applied to any occasion. My goal is for you to learn to create arrangements that go beyond pretty and into the realm of the dramatic, the unexpected, and sometimes even the magical.

Sometimes I wonder whether I would have ever worked in the flower world if I'd grown up in a big city. As luck would have it, I grew up in the country, in a very small village in western Massachusetts. Over the years, I have also lived in bigger, busier places like Brooklyn and Berkeley, California, but I find myself returning to the fields and woods of my childhood for many reasons: peace, fresh air, starlight, and inspiration for my work. Whenever I'm away from the country for too long—designing a wedding in San Francisco or New York, teaching workshops in Amsterdam or Maui, or making bouquets for a photo shoot in Chicago—I long to return to the Berkshire hills, to the place and home where I grew up. The influence of that quiet, river-laced, vine-covered land is all over my soul, and it colors the work I do with plants, flowers, and interiors.

My parents were typical of many couples who moved from New York City to the Berkshires in the early 1970s. They wanted to make things and grow their own food, to be close to the land, and to raise their children in a peaceful place where we would be free to play and explore. My father, Howard Chezar, a carpenter and fine woodworker, built our home by hand with local timber. He designed our kitchen, dining area, and living room as one large space, surrounded by oversized windows, and with so many views and such light that sometimes it seemed as if we lived outdoors. From my earliest days, I remember sitting at our kitchen table staring at trees and miles of fields all the way to Catamount Mountain in the distance.

My mother, Famke Zonneveld, was an artist and teacher who grew up in Indonesia and the Netherlands. Like my father, she loved making things, and she had an innate appreciation for the beauty of the land. In addition to making our home a warm, comforting place, she spent time cooking, gardening, and painting landscapes inspired by the world outside our window. Anything she touched was an extension of her creative self. She encouraged my sister and me to run around outdoors as if it was our very own playroom.

In many ways, that world was also our classroom. My mother, who studied art and later taught at Waldorf Schools, instilled in us a deep

appreciation for art and the natural world. We learned about color and form by constantly drawing from nature. We knew that paper came from trees because she showed us how to make it; we distilled dyes from plants and dipped beeswax candles. Wanting us to have direct experiences with those resources, our mom helped us plant and tend our own little gardens, taught us to sculpt with clay, knit with wool, and bake bread, and even showed us the beauty in something as simple as laundry drying in the sun.

When my city cousins visited, they often said they were bored. My sister and I never were! We got dirty making forts and fairy houses; we pretended to be cooks, using lettuce and comfrey leaves as the "bread" for our make-believe sandwiches. We stalked caterpillars and fireflies and rescued countless wounded birds. Every summer, my mother's Dutch art-school friends came to visit, eager to paint the landscape and portraits of us dressed as fairies or wood nymphs. They marveled at all the raw material we possessed in our own backyard.

Walking among brambles, primroses, and fiddlehead ferns with my sister and our dogs back then was like heaven to me, and it's an activity I now happily share with my own children. The outdoors is still where I feel most at ease. It's where it all comes together, where so many things just seem to make more sense.

My country childhood informs the way I arrange flowers. My goal is always to enhance nature—that's what resonates for me. From my mother and a few other visionaries who made their living by landscape and floral design, I learned how to bring in elements from the outdoors and reinterpret them, to make something beautiful and new while retaining the allure of the wild.

In my desire to capture the wild, I am motivated by a variety of visual elements. Sometimes, for instance, a color calls out to me, inspiring me to create an arrangement. It can happen almost anywhere: when I see pretty fabrics spilling out of my suitcase, a luscious cake in a pastry case, or a superstar flower that seems to call my name. We're all drawn to certain shades, and—no surprise—we tend to like the colors that look good on us. I am fascinated also by the relationship between palettes—the power of contrast and juxtaposition—whether in a clothing combination or, on a larger scale, in the impact of color on a party or wedding I'm designing.

Most often, the flowers themselves motivate my arrangements. I might head to the market in search of one kind of garden rose, but find a gorgeous new carnation that simply takes my breath away. When that happens, I will build my arrangement around this showstopper. I find inspiration, as well, in the luscious abundance of fruits. I like the sculptural element they add, the freedom they allow as I break the traditional "frame" of the bouquet. The grand scale of large branches also inspires, as they allow me the space to create a painterly tableau. Finally, I like working with compotes—footed bowls that allow me to create lush seasonal displays that lift an arrangement but keep it below eye level so it never blocks the view of guests across a table.

To me, working in a lush, painterly style involves two other related components: curating unusual flowers and doing so in their seasons. The life cycle of a plant has an apex, a moment when it is freshest and most replete, when it has a unique life force. For example, tulips in August seem wan and out of place, but late-summer dahlias burst with life. I try to capture that optimal moment in my work, which often leads me to my own garden or to other local growers who complement what I find at the flower market.

I realize not all of us are lucky enough to have such ready resources, but I urge you all to look at what nature has to offer. Sometimes when I want to distinguish a bouquet or elevate an entire look to a grand level, I'll take to the fields or woods. I've often pulled my car to the side of the road because a splash of color caught my eye. There, I'll discover a perfect wild crabapple that will find its way into an evening arrangement. Often, what you are liberating from the roadside are vines and weeds that choke more established plantings. In such cases, your foraging will be welcome. If you are going after something other than a weed, always ask permission.

I like to use branches in intimate as well as large spaces. Working big is a challenge, but once we get the hang of scale (and the right

containers), it becomes easy to master. What are some other constants in my work? Vines! These are the ultimate finishing touch, the one that makes small arrangements span several feet and magically transforms simple bouquets into belles of the ball.

I'm charmed by small, gemlike bouquets in sweet little vessels like julep cups, delicate goblets, and shapely containers. Simple stems can surprise. Every season or so, I find that an overlooked blossom becomes an obsession. At the moment, I cannot get enough carnations into my work. For years, I have been mad for all species of fritillaria, especially the checkered lily, *Fritillaria meleagris*, a tiny, burgundy checkerboard of a flower that blooms from bulbs in early spring. During their short window, I use them in almost every arrangement. Also, keep in mind that single varieties of almost any flower grouped together, unadorned, can make a big impression.

Some flowers capture your attention and refuse to let go. Walk into a room where a single peony reposes in a glass, and you are mesmerized by the sheer mass of its frilly petals and saturated color. Pointy golden tulips make it seem as if spring just invited you on a date. Stare into a gardenia's creamy face, and marvel at how it looks like porcelain. Inside a plain white tent for a wedding reception, find a magical green grotto, lavish with bright ferns, cool moss, and pale orchids, and you are transported to the tropics.

There are some arrangements I return to again and again, each time using seasonal flowers and inspired accents to create something unique. For party tabletops, I'm fond of compotes. In springtime, I let them brim with checkered lilies, hellebores, and trailing akebia vines. In another season, I might use the same container filled with peonies and dogwood. For high-ceilinged spaces, no matter what the season, I often begin with blossoming tree limbs in a heavy urn, which, by the way, I urge everyone to invest in. Put one in your living room or entryway, and you'll be surprised how much fun it is to fill every month with long-lasting branches. For hand-tied bouquets, I like to create "little worlds," clustering loose blooms like peonies and garden roses alongside tight buds and something fluttery like clematis. Whatever I'm working on, I try to keep the concept of handcrafted in mind.

The hypnotic pleasure of plants and flowers still astonishes me. We call upon them to make special occasions even more momentous. Their abundant beauty enhances our surroundings, reminding us that just being alive is worth celebrating. Though the finished pieces are ephemeral, working with flowers can be every bit as satisfying as painting a watercolor or crafting a piece of furniture. Choosing and placing each element with care makes me feel as deliberate and devoted to a fine result as a jeweler, woodworker, or pastry chef. With this book, I'd like to deepen our shared knowledge of this craft and honor its practitioners. And I'd love to help you create the glorious, fragrant, flowing profusion that's destined for your next celebration. I hope you'll accept my invitation.

The art of painterly arrangements

The process of making a flower arrangement involves many of the same principles that go into making fine art, and that's why the term *painterly* is a fitting way to describe my style of arranging. I can remember standing, transfixed, in front of Monet's famous water lilies at New York's Museum of Modern Art. Just as the artist's thick brushstrokes and use of color create that lily pond, you can bring movement to your flower arrangements by building tone upon tone of similar colors.

To achieve this sense of movement, make use of the painterly concept of chiaroscuro, Italian for "clear-obscure" or "light-dark." Using this technique, painters like Caravaggio, a master of the Italian Baroque, contrasted dramatic highlights with mysteriously dim backgrounds. In floral design, when you combine flowers of the same color—but in varying shades, ranging from light to dark—your arrangements will acquire similar depth. The eye will naturally move from light to shadow, which heightens the impact of the blossoms.

No floral images remain more compelling than those painted in the Netherlands during the seventeenth century. This was the golden age of science, when plant hunters circled the globe, and scholars began to codify the botanical world. Floral still lifes became the rage, and artists took great pride in getting every stamen, leaf striation, and petal correct. Often, these elaborate botanical portraits would include bees, butterflies, and hummingbirds. The result was a magnificent moment in time, a snapshot of perfection, and it's this arresting beauty that I want to capture in my arrangements.

If you study Dutch still-life paintings, you'll observe that the flowers vary in color, shape, and size, even as vines tumble, wrap, and trail. This is the kind of wild, romantic style that can make an arrangement so appealing. But, that said, you need to impose order onto even a seemingly untamed creation by balancing color with texture, seasonality, foliage, and foraged elements.

Start with color

When you begin planning an arrangement, the choices can be overwhelming. There is so much variety available. How do you narrow your selections? Color is your first filter.

If you are shopping for a special event, such as a wedding or dinner, don't buy until you have a color scheme. Perusing your garden or visiting flower shops or a flower market during this decision-making process will give you a better sense of what's available and the potential costs. You'll also want to consult your mood board (page 41). Once you've decided, stick with that palette. No wandering into purples or mauves when your goal is green and white.

As a rule, it's best to design with one or two main colors in mind. You may feel a spring day calls for sunny yellows or peaches, and an evening dinner begs for purples and blues. Or perhaps the season demands peonies, a flower that almost defines early summer. I have often let one perfect blossom decide my color direction.

Either way, color is your first control. When you have chosen that, you can focus without distraction on flower selection, building on a variety of tones, textures, and shapes until the arrangement has many layers and striking depth.

How do you choose your color pairings? You can opt for analogous shades, those located close together on the color wheel: purples and blues, for example, or reds and pinks. Or you can choose to riff on opposite shades, for example, the striking way that burgundy blossoms contrast with pale yellow.

The selective use of color gives you great freedom with flower forms. You can play with shapes, combining a buxom peony, a round ranunculus, and a slender lily in the same arrangement as long as they echo a similar shade and tone. Ultimately, you are attempting to instill a sense of movement in your designs with color, shape, and texture. Each arrangement draws the eye through the subtle shifts of color, creating an engaging and compelling effect.

Design with foliage—the secret ingredient

Here's a task I often present to my workshop students: design
an arrangement made entirely of foliage. Add berries, fruits, and
vines—but no flowers. The results are often electric. Students mix an
assortment of fuzzy geranium leaves with textured mint; they combine
the soft chartreuse of linden pods with papery copper beech leaves.
Searching out color, they find beauty in branches of red dogwood,
rust tones in the turning leaves of oakleaf hydrangea, and gold in the
berries of viburnum. The point of this exercise is to demonstrate the
importance of foliage, which adds texture, movement, and character
to any arrangement.

Since green acts as a neutral in floral design, leaves, seedpods, vines,
and other greenery provide visual interest without distracting. Think of
still-green fruits or hellebores in the spring, Russian olive or clematis vine
in the summer, akebia vines and dogwood in the fall. There is no end to
the variety of textures green provides: wispy grasses, twisting vines, bold
leaves, dramatic branches. Each adds more layers, more texture, to an
arrangement while creating a backdrop for bolder colors.

Foliage can even take center stage as autumn approaches. "How beautiful
the leaves grow old," writes naturalist John Burroughs. "How full of light
and color are their last days." Indeed, foliage that changes color with
the seasons can be a cherished addition to your arrangements. Each leaf
seems its own work of art. Look for branches that are transitioning from
green to pink to burgundy. Nature has a perfect eye for color, and your
job is simply to follow its lead.

Finally, don't ignore the backs of leaves. Magnolia leaves are two-toned—
green on the front, brown on the back—and often the reverse side adds
another dimension to a design. The same is true of the silver-gray of Russian
olive, which sets off the strong hues of flowers in fuchsias and pinks.

Find your focus

Always search for focal flowers, one or several blossoms that anchor a design and give it a dramatic presence. Any blossom can be a focal flower, but there are some constants that seldom disappoint. Tree peonies, with their extraordinary range of shades, are an excellent focal flower. Tulips can be a focal flower, especially the Parrot varieties, which look as if fairies have painted them. Also consider amaryllis, ranunculus, roses, and dahlias. Each produces blossoms that simply "stop traffic." Because of their size, color, and shape, or a combination, you cannot take your eyes off them. Sometimes I go to the market sure of the exact flower I'm seeking. Just as often, I'm surprised by a flower I haven't thought of, and though I seldom change my color scheme, I do incorporate unexpected finds.

Sometimes you can use a focal flower on its own: giant dahlias coursing down a dinner table, each in its own vase (see page 225). In a more complex arrangement, the focal flower, or flowers, should capture the eye. Think, for example, of a collection of yellow roses at the peak of bloom accented with red raspberry canes and branches laden with ripening peaches (see page 136). When they are nestled next to each other, the roses add softness and movement to the arrangement, and the peaches convey an undeniable abundance.

Think texture

Contrast is an essential part of creating arrangements with a natural look. Bold, spiky dahlias have even greater impact, for example, when set beside the delicate fluttering of a Japanese anemone. Similarly, a crisp white freesia contrasts beautifully with a shiny orange mandarin. Let berries brush up against branches, or snuggle fluffy blooms next to tight buds. Remember to consider not only the flower, but also the fruit. Boughs of just-ripening apricots or raspberry canes add fantastic and unusual textures to arrangements. Make wreaths of red peppers, or gather eggplants and tomatillos to create still lifes on the dining table. Add a spiky artichoke. Seek beauty in the juxtaposition of rough and smooth.

Source seasonally and locally

The one thing more beautiful than a dahlia in full bloom is a dahlia you have grown yourself. That's among the reasons I've found such delight in the ninety-acre farm my husband, Chris, and I purchased in 2012 in Ghent, New York.

Located twenty minutes from our Berkshire home, the old farm provides an abundance of material for my work. I've discovered old apple trees, wild dogwood and witch hazel, marvelous ferns, and all manner of vines on the property.

Chris and I have planted an orchard—crabapples, plums, and apricots that we raise as much for their flowers as their fruit. I also grow woody shrubs—plants whose leaves and flowers I use in my work. I've put together a list of shrubs, perennials, and annuals you might consider growing to use in your own flower arranging (page 55).

Finally, we cleared a field close to the old farmhouse to hold a hoop house, about the size of two basketball courts. Early tulips grace the beds, followed by majestic Darwin hybrids, and colorful Parrots. When those bulbs are removed in the spring, we grow sweet peas, cup-and-saucer vines, and row upon row of dahlias. In the outdoor fields, I sow zinnias and marigolds in varieties that are seldom found in the market.

Zonneveld Farm is named for my mother—whose maiden name means "sunny field" in Dutch. She would have loved this farm and shared my vision for it as a place to teach workshops and harvest my own flowers.

Fortunately, like me, a growing number of farmer/florists want to lower the carbon footprint of the flowers we use. Growers who sell to the public are easy to locate. If you have a local farmers' market, chances are you can find a seller who specializes in flowers. You can also log on to slowflowers.com, an organization developed by Seattle writer and slow-flower pioneer Debra Prinzing. The site has links to flower farmers all over the United States.

CONTINUED ON PAGE 26

A TRIP TO THE FLOWER MARKET

Although you should strive to source flowers locally—or grow them yourself—visiting a wholesale flower market is a magical experience. It's a little like falling down the rabbit hole. You can't believe there are so many beautiful flowers in the world.

Most flower markets are reticent about do-it-yourselfers. These are wholesale establishments that service designers and florists who have a tax ID number, and they are not as interested in selling to the public. However, most will allow buyers later in the day, after their regular customers have shopped. Check in advance to see what hours retail shoppers are welcome. You will most likely have to pay any applicable tax on your purchases, and it's best to pay in cash.

Wherever you shop, set a budget before you go. It's better to choose wisely than to come home with expensive flowers you don't need.

Have a plan. Here's where a mood board comes into play (page 41). What's your occasion? What's your color scheme? Will you have small bouquets or large ones? Have you thought about boutonnieres and table flowers? Know what kind of vessels you'll be using. Check the calendar; use flowers that are in season (page 232).

Reconnoiter. If you are shopping for a wedding or other special event, visit the market days or weeks before you make any purchases. Scope out the scene, talk to wholesalers, and suss out which ones are willing to work with you. Check prices so you can keep to your floral budget. Do not select specific flowers at this time, since the flower selection may change by the time you return. Rather, your goal is to see how the flower market works, connect with dealers, and see the kinds of prices that they charge.

CONTINUED

Dress warmly. Most of the spaces you visit will be refrigerated to a temperature that is more comfortable for flowers than humans.

Shop three or four days in advance. If your wedding or special event is on a Saturday, it's best to shop the market on a Wednesday or Thursday. Talk to your vendors about which blooms will open on time and which may open too quickly. Most vendors will let you place your selections on an open shelf so you don't have to wander about laden with bulky purchases.

Be flexible and welcome inspiration. Some wholesalers may be willing to place an advance order for you—they may even offer a discount because you are buying in bulk. However, on the day you arrive to pick up your flowers, don't be surprised if some items aren't available. Weather, transport, and timing can wreak havoc on even the best design schemes. A good vendor will suggest alternatives. Better yet, take a look around. Is there a rose that inspires you, a lily you've never seen before? It's rare that I leave the flower market without something new and exciting.

Shop for more than flowers. You'll find good prices on all sorts of floral tools and resources: vases, frogs, wire, clippers, and votives, as well as potted plants. I buy spectacular begonias in pots, knowing I will clip them to use in arrangements. This is also the place to look for flowering branches and all manner of trailing vines. If there is a blossoming tree out there, you can bet that someone has harvested the branches for the flower market.

Hydrate and condition. Make sure you have buckets of fresh water for transporting your purchases. If you are buying large branches, set them into a small bucket filled with just enough water to submerge the ends, then place that bucket into a larger container— perhaps a garbage can—to keep water from sloshing into your vehicle.

Flowers grown in season are bursting with a life force that may be missing from blooms raised half a world away. More to the point, there's an awful lot of beautiful material growing where you live, such as unusual foliage and vines. Forage in your own backyard or on your street.

What you find in your backyard or on a local farm depends on the time of year and geography. I include a seasonal list of go-to blooms (page 232) to help with planning. In addition, each arrangement in this book is labeled by season and, whenever possible, suggests alternate choices that allow you to tailor the design for other seasons.

Forage for the unexpected

"In nature, nothing is perfect and everything is perfect," writes novelist Alice Walker. I agree wholeheartedly. I've found wild grapevines contorted in shapes I could never reproduce, fiddlehead ferns unfurling with the day, and spiky chestnuts still green on the tree. Take advantage of generous gifts like these. They are nothing you can plan, but they can make all the difference between an ordinary arrangement and one that turns heads.

I'm fortunate that I can forage for berries, ferns, or other flora on my own farm. This corner of New England also is ripe with old orchards that are handy for harvesting when the trees erupt in blooms. There is potential everywhere. Even in winter, not the most floral of seasons, you'll discover an abundance of natural treasures—from bare branches and moss to vibrant berries still clinging to the vine. I wander through my garden and find red-twig dogwood, yellow-striped weeping willow, and all manner of evergreens.

If you live in a city and foraging means going to your local flower or farmers' market, the principles are the same. It's just a bit more fun when you discover unexpected treasures. If the blossoms and branches you covet belong to someone, don't hesitate to stop and ring the doorbell. I've done it often and politely offered to pay for a sprig of this or that. Sometimes, the offer is accepted; often, people are delighted to contribute

an armload of lilac or witch hazel without compensation. I usually leave with the flowers *and* a new friend.

A few years ago, on one of my first trips to the Hawaiian Islands, I saw a vine with orange tubular flowers, *Pyrostegia venusta*, covering a residential enclosure. When I knocked on the door, the sweetest woman answered; she was more than happy to let me walk away with armloads of that stunning vine. Later, it graced the table of a wedding I was working on. The vine proved to be the element that brought everything together.

Allow for Abundance

How do you achieve generous, full-blown arrangements without breaking the bank? One option is to mix inexpensive blooms with a few dynamite focal flowers. Zinnias and carnations are inexpensive, for example. Pair them with just the right rose or a giant dahlia, and you have liftoff. Partner narcissus with orchids, ranunculus with Parrot tulips, carnations with garden roses. The less expensive blooms can be used abundantly, forming large clusters in an arrangement. The more expensive focal flowers should be used sparingly. Blooming branches are always a good addition. Dogwood, fruit blossoms, spirea, and viburnum are dramatic. Anything you've gathered from your garden comes with the best price tag of all: absolutely free.

Vases, Vessels, and Other Containers

Any container that holds water can hold flowers: coffeepots, cans, apothecary jars, antique pewter vessels, glass compotes, and concrete urns. If you are drawn to a container that doesn't hold water, such as a porous wooden box, a wicker basket, or a rusty sap bucket, conceal a plastic yogurt container or glass jar inside your vessel and build from there.

Tall cylindrical vases might work for longer stems, like tulips, but they don't lend themselves to fuller arrangements. Instead, look for footed vessels, like compotes or urns that are wider at the top.

It's best to match your container to the mood of an event. A casual, country-style reception might call for mason jars, water pitchers, or ceramic pots. A more formal celebration could use silver-plated tea sets, fancy pedestal bowls, or crystal goblets.

Narrow-necked bottles and bud vases are good for single stems and can be arranged in groups. They can wander down a dinner table or sit at every place setting. Silver tea services, with their matching sugar bowls and cream pitchers are great for a table featuring a large arrangement and two smaller satellite pieces. Beakers, flasks, and other laboratory glassware are striking, modern containers. Haunt tag sales and flea markets for period pieces that are as unique as the arrangements that will fill them.

Now that you have a good understanding of the design principles, the next step is to explore the techniques and tools necessary for creating a dramatic arrangement. Since flowers are a fragile art form, it's important to treat them well. What follow are the essentials that I teach in all my flower workshops. Once students understand these basics, they can create all the arrangements in this book. More importantly, they will be able to improvise and develop new arrangements of their own.

Essential techniques and tools

Techniques

Certain techniques can be employed in preparing and constructing a flower arrangement regardless of its size and content. If you want your arrangements to last, the flowers must be properly conditioned as soon as you bring them home. Once you are ready to create an arrangement, there are several basic steps that will help you achieve your vision.

Condition and Hydrate

The key ingredient for good floral maintenance is water. Supply lots of it and be sure your flowers are prepped to absorb as much as they can (see "Trim, Then Trim Again," below). If you are shopping at a flower market, travel with a bucket and a half-gallon jug of water, or at least enough water to fill your container half full. If you are cutting flowers in your garden, carry along a bucket of water. When planning a big event, it's best to let flowers sit overnight in a cool spot so they become conditioned to the environment and absorb as much water as possible. After the rest, they will be less traumatized and open their buds to reveal added color and detail.

Trim, Then Trim Again

Cut flower stems when you bring them home, and cut them again immediately before you add them to a vase. It's best to cut on a diagonal, which exposes more of the stem to water.

Branches or woody stems should be crosscut with an X at the bottom to allow for more water intake (if they are narrow, a single slice will do). When preparing hyacinths, tulips, irises, or other bulbs, be sure to cut off the hard white section at the bottom of the stem so that water can be more readily absorbed. Place the stem in cold water after cutting. For poppies, scorch the stem by burning the tip with a match or lighter, or dip in scalding water. Poppies ooze a kind of sticky sap, and they last a lot longer in water if the ends are sealed.

Cut away all excess foliage. Leaves often suck up water, so unless they will be featured in your work, remove them when you first trim the branches. Likewise, remove all leaves that may fall below the water level so they do not decay and soil the water.

Prepare your vessel

If you are using a vase or vessel that doesn't hold water, find a smaller waterproof container and slip it inside the vase. If you are using a floral frog or another form of anchor, affix it to the bottom of your container with floral putty. Fill containers three-quarters full with cold water and start adding flowers. If you want to force tightly closed flower heads so they open fully and faster, use warm water instead. Warm water is suitable for rose or peony buds and for oriental lilies. Lilacs also prefer warm water.

Don't rush while arranging

This is the fun part! If you're not getting the look you want, start again. When stymied, wander into your backyard for inspiration. Clip a branch here, a bunch of greenery there. Take your time and let the beauty of the blossoms guide you.

Cut to fit

As a rule, your tallest branch or flower stem should be about one and a half times the height of the vase you are using. That said, this is a rule that is made to be broken. My workshop students are often amazed when I cut a flower stem to 3 or 4 inches, placing the short flowers—or fruits and berries—along the edge of the container. This breaks the line of the vase and creates a more painterly, organic effect.

HOW TO MAKE A BASE LAYER

To construct an arrangement, first position your tallest branches in the form of an inverted triangle. This upside-down pyramid shape creates a structure that guarantees your finished arrangement will have a horizontal presence as well as a vertical one. Although you will most often begin your arrangements with a trio of branches, you may sometimes use more. For consistency, I will refer to this beginning step as the base layer in the recipes that follow.

• If the arrangement is to be placed against a wall, the base layer will be slightly more vertical, with one branch positioned straight up in the back center, another arching to the left, and the third bending to the right.

• If the arrangement is to be placed on a dining table, the base layer should be more horizontal. You want diners to be able to see over the arrangement. For a horizontal base layer, position three branches arching outward over the edge of the vase roughly at 12 o'clock, 3 o'clock, and 9 o'clock.

• If you have more than one type of branch, trim, clip, and add those, either interspersing them with the first branches or resting them on top of the first branches. You are, in fact, creating multiple base layers. The goal is to make a balanced framework for whatever flowers come next.

• Once the basic architecture is established, add smaller branches and foliage, always keeping the same inverted triangle in mind.

Arrange in size order

Work from large to small. Anchor large branches first in a base layer (page 37), then position your focal flowers by placing the stems into frogs or whatever grid you have created. If your arrangement is to be viewed from all sides, the focal flowers should be placed so they can be viewed from every angle. If your arrangement is to be located against a wall, don't waste important flowers far in the back, where they won't be seen. Rather than placing your focal flowers dead center, arrange them slightly to one side or another—this is another trick borrowed from the painter's quiver. Fill any holes with greenery, a dainty branch, or smaller, accent flowers.

Finally, add floaters, those wispy little blossoms that hover above a finished arrangement. If you'd like to wrap a vine around the pedestal of a vase, anchor and wrap that first, then proceed with the rest of the arrangement. At other times, you can finish with a vine, securing it into the frog and weaving it around and through other branches and flowers.

Observe the rule of three

The Latin saying *omne trium perfectum*—"everything that comes in threes is perfect"—is an important floral mantra. An arrangement of three looks more natural and less forced than an even-numbered collection. Group three pots of orchids, for example, or three amaryllis bulbs, or three tiny vases on a windowsill. You can apply this same rule when constructing an arrangement. Cluster small blossoms in groups of three—or five— so they make a strong impression and create a balance of symmetry and asymmetry.

Fine-tune blossoms

Edit ruthlessly. Flowers are beautiful, but they aren't perfect. Consider each branch and stem, looking for ways to improve its appearance. For example, you'll want to remove any buds that detract from the impact of a single flower. Eliminate outside petals that are less than perfect; trim leaves that compete for water; peel away the papery brown sheaths from a budding daffodil. Often, large branches require thinning, either of faded blossoms or of empty twigs. Like a sculptor, you are trying to remove anything that inhibits dramatic impact.

MAKING A
MOOD BOARD

When you plan a large-scale project, such as a wedding or a similar celebration, it's wise to prepare a mood board. This is a type of collage consisting of images, colors, and styles that will provide inspiration and help develop your aesthetic. You can construct a mood board online using a Pinterest app (and you can find many examples there that might inspire you), but having a physical object allows you to live with the mood board and reflect on it over time. The colors will look different at different times of day, and your preferences and feelings may change depending on which room you place the mood board.

• Purchase a sheet of white foam core board at an office supply store in any size you wish.

• Start posting on the board whatever inspires you: magazine clippings, color swatches, bits of ribbon, pictures of table settings, and family photographs. Add items that reflect the feeling you are trying to convey.

• Use the mood board to help you concentrate your ideas. Don't be too specific. This is not the place to compose flower lists or count compotes. The best art is often made in the moment. Plan ahead, by all means, but don't lock yourself into a rigid vision that narrows your choices.

Keep it cool

Once an arrangement is completed, make sure it is placed in a cool space. Check the water level frequently. You might be surprised at how much flowers drink.

Tools

In addition to the tools mentioned below, which are available online or at floral supply or craft stores, flower arranging requires the same arsenal of tools that reside in any garden shed or at a good garden supply store. If you're cutting branches, you'll need a well-sharpened saw and loppers. Gardening gloves are helpful outdoors—long ones if you're collecting thorny berry canes, short ones if you're harvesting flowers.

Anchors

For small arrangements, a vase might be tall enough to hold flowers without an anchor. But for larger arrangements, anchors like flower frogs are essential. Flower frogs are designed to sit at the bottom of a vase or bowl and hold flower stems in place. They come in a wide variety of shapes and sizes; some look like metal pin cushions; others look like toothbrush holders. More elaborate, antique frogs might take the shape of a bird, fish, or toad and are highly collectible. Made of metal, plastic, or glass, these frogs are designed to hold even the trickiest flower arrangement firmly in place.

My favorite anchors are spiky *pin frogs*. These are generally metal and available in sizes to fit large or small containers. The sharp, pointed pins look like the proverbial "bed of nails" and are reliable for anchoring small stems that are impaled on the spikes and thus held upright. *Cage frogs* also come in a variety of sizes and have holes that larger stems fit into so that each branch is separately supported and will stay where it's placed. Whichever type you select, always anchor your frog to the bottom of the vase with *floral putty*. Floral putty is malleable yet sticky enough to adhere to surfaces. It is designed to secure floral anchors in a vase or other dish. The putty prevents movement of a floral frog so an

arrangement retains its form. (If you have trouble removing floral putty after an event, just pour some vegetable oil over it, let it rest for five minutes, and it will be easier to lift off.)

You can make your own cage frog by balling up a piece of chicken wire and stuffing it into a vase. The wire will hold stems and help keep them in position, but a frog is ideal and a worthwhile investment.

Some designers prefer *floral foam* to anchor flowers, but I seldom use it. This is a petroleum-based product that doesn't decompose. Because you can anchor a branch or stem anywhere on the foam, its use can produce some very artificial-looking arrangements (like spokes on a bicycle wheel).

Buckets

I never go anywhere, not even to the supermarket, without a bucket in my car. Five-gallon plastic buckets with handles are helpful for harvesting flowers and branches from your garden. You can recycle buckets once used for spackle or plaster, or haunt bakeries for buckets that once held frosting. Taller plastic buckets designed to keep flowers upright are easy for transporting blossoms from a flower market and are available through most floral supply stores. Flowers need water to survive, so always fill the bottom of your buckets. Clean buckets with bleach between uses.

Floral wire and floral tape

Floral wire is flexible aluminum wire that is often coated with a layer of colored paint. Use a shade of green to help it blend in with foliage. The wire is measured in thickness, or gauge; the lower the gauge, the thicker and less pliable the wire (for example, 16 gauge is thicker than 32 gauge). Floral wire, sold by the foot, is often packaged in spools (or paddles). You can use paddle wire to add greenery or fruits when constructing a wreath or draping a chandelier, or wherever long lengths of wire are required for attaching blossoms. Floral wire is also sold in precut pieces called *stem wire*, since it is most often used to wrap around fragile stems that need extra support. Stem wire is also used to wrap flowers for boutonnieres.

Floral tape is a self-sealing tape, available in various colors, which can be used to wrap the stems in a bouquet or a previously wired boutonniere. Available in a half-inch width, the tape is also used to create tape grids on wide-mouthed vases (similar to a lattice crust on a cherry pie) in order to help anchor an arrangement. This technique is best with short, rounded arrangements that will hide the tape from view. Sometimes, with a particularly wide vessel, it may be best to combine a flower frog and a taped grid.

Lazy Susan

A lazy Susan is especially useful for making a table arrangement because you can turn the container as you work to be sure you are considering your design from all angles. You can find a variety of lazy Susans at most kitchen stores. Select one that is big enough to hold the weight of a large flower arrangement.

Pruning shears and scissors

Pruning shears are a crucial tool, both in the field and in the flower studio. These clippers are strong enough to cut tree branches up to 1-inch thick. (For bigger branches, you'll need loppers, which are a larger, two-handed, longer-handled version of pruning shears.) Bypass shears are pruning shears with one narrow, convex blade and a wider, concave one, and they are most useful for cutting between branches. For thinning branches, you'll find needle-nose, scissorlike shears more useful.

I recommend two brands, Felco and Chikamasa. Felco pruning shears are sturdy and reliable. They come in seventeen different styles, including designs for left-handed gardeners. The original Felco, known as Felco F-2 bypass shears, are a good place to start.

When preparing an arrangement in the studio, I always carry Chikamasa T-600 Almighty Shears in a leather holster on my belt (you'll find the holsters in any good garden store). These shears are pointed, more like heavy scissors, and are excellent for snipping away extra buds or trimming back foliage. I also use Chikamasa B-300 carbon steel scissors when I need to do fine trimming of smaller flowers and foliage.

Other assorted tools

You will want *rubber bands* for fastening the stems of handheld bouquets and a box of straight *corsage pins* to pin boutonnieres to lapels or fasten bouquet ribbons. A *glue gun*, available in any craft store, is useful for attaching ribbons. *Plastic tubes* that hold water for individual blossoms look like chemistry set test tubes. Each has a rubber top that allows for a single flower to be set into the tube. The tubes are useful if you need to fasten flowers on a garland around a door or on a chandelier where other water options are not available.

A *candle* or *lighter* is necessary for sealing the sap in a poppy stem, and a *thorn stripper* is essential for removing thorns from roses or berry vines so they won't catch on other branches. A *sharp knife* comes in handy for whittling the end of a branch to fit better into a cage frog. Victorinox, makers of the Swiss Army knife, also make a 4-inch floral knife that's easy to use. Always have *tissue paper* and a variety of beautiful *ribbons* on hand for wrapping bouquets.

"More than anything, I must have flowers always, always," said Claude Monet. On the grayest winter day, I wake to a small vase of grape hyacinth sitting on my bedside table and feel content. I can't imagine a simpler route to joy than filling a home with flowers.

This chapter is about the quotidian: the moments that don't demand elaborate arrangements but, when filled with flowers, make our day that much more special. There are many ways you can include more flowers in your life. For example, the bay window in my kitchen faces east. I raise tuberous begonias there, delighting in both leaf and bloom. I'll take cuttings of my favorite leaf and root them in tiny vases. From time to time, those will be potted up and delivered to favorite friends. In winter, I'll add pots of mini-cyclamen to my window nook.

We all have favorite spots that catch our eye and call for floral embellishment. Scent is one way to determine location. A dozen purple-blue freesias on a night table might do the trick in spring. In winter, I'm a fool for narcissus. Plant lilies of the valley in your backyard—they spread with abandon—and you'll soon have bouquets that smell of summer. Fill a bowl with decorative quinces, set it by your bed, and inhale their perfume before you go to sleep.

Bathrooms are a great location for potted ferns: the warm mist of the shower will keep them green and thriving on a windowsill. Orchids also flourish in moist air. They can fill an indoor window box that hangs near the medicine cabinet and elegantly carry you through a cold, gray winter.

Sometimes, my flowers come from the local supermarket. I'll buy pots of colorful primroses, three at a time. Just remove the flowers from their plastic pots and sink the trio into a wooden trough placed on the dinner table. When the flowers finally fade, you can replant the primroses in an outdoor border and wait for a second spring of bloom.

What else do I find in the local market? Miniature daffodils, also in groups of three, that make their way into a ceramic planter I bought in Mexico. Orchids! Purchase a handful of tiny, baby orchids and replant each in a tiny, white, footed compote. They can saunter down a sideboard

Living with flowers

or decorate a cheese platter. Or take a half-dozen pink cymbidium orchids, place them in a shallow white bowl, and cover the planting medium with moss liberated from a damp rock you discovered on an evening walk.

In fact, a walk in the woods can yield all manner of interesting tablescapes. My daughter and I, inveterate collectors, often come home from our rambles with a collection of turkey feathers or a fallen bird's nest that begs for display. Add some seasonal fruit, a handful of nuts in the shell and you capture a memory even as you decorate your dining room table.

There are always flowers on that table, whether my family is dining alone or with friends. As winter fades, there will be simple arrangements of tulips or narcissus as a centerpiece. In summer, I'll take a morning walk through the garden, snipping perfect blooms as I wander. I don't fuss over their arranging. I welcome the simplicity of a bouquet composed of a single variety of flower. When dining at a friend's home, surprise your host with a pretty arrangement to grace a table of hors d'oeuvres. No cheeseboard should go unadorned, I say, especially when you can

clip a handful of blooming rosemary from the garden or garnish a platter with nasturtiums.

Spring provides the gift of blooming branches. This is when you pull out your tall vases and fill them full of forsythia or flowering quince. Cut these shrubs just as they bud and you can force the season to explode weeks early. In the dining or living room, fashion an impromptu swag to peek over a framed mirror.

Summer is all about the flower garden. Simply sprinkle a packet of cosmos seeds onto damp soil, and you'll have a summer's worth of blooms to fashion into bouquets. Better still, plant a peony hedge, one that features an early bloomer like 'Abalone Pearl', blush pink and white, and 'Etched Salmon', a double rose type that blooms midseason. Throw in the late-blooming 'Festiva Maxima', and you'll have blossoms that last from May to late June.

Don't despair when fall arrives. Instead, look at all the decorative gifts nature presents. I harvest the dried seedheads of my alliums and, placing them in narrow bud vases, line them up along the fireplace mantle. Hydrangeas are the gift that keeps on giving; they are beautiful in shades of pink and white when they are fresh and dramatic as dried arrangements gathered in a giant vase. I've only once regretted my fall harvests; that was the year I collected milkweed seedpods, bursting with white "fluff." The silky, white seeds looked like angel hair on the family Christmas tree, but they also scooted into every nook and cranny of my house. I still vacuum up these "holiday treats" every time I clean.

In winter, order bulbs as gifts for friends. Buy terra-cotta pots and in each plant one or a trio of amaryllis bulbs surrounded by a circle of moss. My current favorites are 'Naranja', a bold orange, and 'Double Record', a double white amaryllis edged with red.

Living with flowers can be an everyday pleasure. Keep a collection of vases on hand (canning jars are great for holding flowers on their way to your neighbor's dinner party), step into your garden to greet the day or stop at a local market, and keep your color scheme simple.

GROW YOUR OWN

Anyone with a small backyard can grow an abundance of flowering branches and colorful shrubs to fashion a season's worth of arrangements. Trees and shrubs are especially easy to grow. Just dig a good hole, plant, feed, and water, and you'll have plenty of branches to accent the roses, carnations, amaryllis, ranunculus, or other flowers you purchase.

Here are some classics that I have planted on my farm. If you live in warmer climes, you can add jasmine and camellias. Consult a local garden center to fine-tune this list by region.

- Trees: plum, apricot, peach, crabapple, copper beech, dogwood, magnolia

- Shrubs: smoke bush, lilac, viburnum, forsythia, hydrangea, boxwood, flowering quince

- Vines: wisteria, multiple varieties of clematis, sweet pea, love in a puff, ivy, grapevine, akebia, cup-and-saucer

- Perennials: delphinium, hellebore, bearded iris, lavender, lily, poppy, peony, tree peony, lily of the valley, hosta, foxglove, coral bells for foliage

- Annuals: zinnia, dahlia, cosmos, snapdragon, annual poppy

- Bulbs: daffodil, tulip, allium, common hyacinth, fritillaria, grape hyacinth

Tonal arrangements

Observe the play of light on a flower garden in the late afternoon. The harsh colors of midday fade and in their place are a multitude of shades and tones. Depending on how the shadows fall, a single rose bush may appear blush pink or deep fuchsia, or a tulip may transition from sunset orange to soft coral. This is the way nature plays with color, and you should try to incorporate that same flirtation of light and dark into your floral designs.

The secret is to limit your color palette. When I pick flowers for my own home, I often gather just one type of blossom—a bunch of white cosmos, for example, or a handful of red poppies. A single mass of any flower provides strong, graphic impact and is one way to show a humble garden flower to its best advantage. Gather too many colors into one bouquet, and there is no place for the eye to rest.

For more sophisticated arrangements, pick two colors (never more than three) and, using green as a neutral, build on the theme by adding multiples of the same shade. You might select pink garden roses, pink ranunculus, and pink tulips—each blossom in a similar shade but a different shape or texture. This extends the color and adds depth, seducing the eye to look—and look again.

You can also work with neighbors on the color wheel: varieties of pink and orange or soft greens and blues. Sometimes, let yourself be lured by opposites: yellow with burgundy, for example (dark colors cut the sweetness of light ones). An easy option for novice designers is to use varying shades of green and white, which are always classic. Or try apricot and peach tones, which can transition in one direction toward yellow, in another toward champagne.

The great beauty of flowers is that a single variety can contain gradations of the same or similar colors: multicolor Parrot tulips, for example, or the majestic tree peony. These are nature's gift to the floral arranger, and they make ideal focal flowers—the ones that anchor an arrangement. You can also draw raves with the less dramatic picotee carnation, a two-tone blossom that adds depth and quiet drama to an arrangement of modern roses.

To further heighten the impact of a tonal arrangement, adapt a painterly technique called ombré. Think of the undulations of color in a J. M. W. Turner canvas, or the way a John Singer Sargent watercolor shifts gradually from one color to another or from light to dark. Keep this concept in mind when you want to give a two-color arrangement a sense of movement. Several examples are presented later in this chapter.

Finally, some tips on containers. When you play with color, your vessel can add the final accent or unbalance a carefully created assemblage. For an arrangement with shades from soft peach to burgundy, try a clear glass container that lets the flowers dominate. If you are after more drama, use pewter or silver, which adds a level of sophistication.

Bold red

Red is the color of passion and desire. It's a strong color that makes a bold statement. Fortunately, it appears frequently in the flower world. A red tulip is glorious; a Parrot tulip just about perfect. To reinforce the essence of spring, add a variety of red ranunculus. The black-faced red anemone, with its dark center, is just the right foil, drawing the eye farther into the arrangement. The blowsy, open quality of Parrot tulips inspires an arrangement that aims for a light, airy effect. Each tulip is a star, so you want it to have room to impress. You can choose a variety of vines to weave through the flowers, but the furry stems of the thornless blackberry echo the color red.

ALTERNATE FLOWERS In summer, use roses; in fall, dahlias; in winter, amaryllis.

1 This vase is tall enough so you don't need to use a frog. Fill three-quarters full with water.

2 Remove excess foliage from the Parrot tulips. Trim them so they stand 6 to 12 inches above the lip of the vase. Place the tulips in the vase, allowing them to arch out in every direction.

3 Trim the ranunculus and anemones to about the same height, and position them in groups of two or three. The goal is to have an uncrowded arrangement that alternates between the tonal qualities of each blossom. Trim the standard tulips to a similar length and intersperse them among the other flowers.

4 Trim the blackberry vines and feed them into the vase so that each winds through and around the flowers. Larger leaves should hang over the lip of the vase; smaller ones can wrap up and into the arrangement. Trim and add the jasmine sprigs for accent.

FOOTED GLASS VASE, MEDIUM

15 RED PARROT TULIPS

7 RED RANUNCULUS

10 BLACK-FACED RED ANEMONES

3 STANDARD RED TULIPS

5 THORNLESS BLACKBERRY VINES

3 JASMINE SPRIGS

Bright orange

Orange can bend in many directions, toward autumnal hues or the soft light of dawn. It can pop or recede. This arrangement is inspired by 'Avignon', a dramatic Parrot tulip developed by Dutch breeders. Varying from cantaloupe to sunset to citrus, it pairs well with kumquats, also popular in the spring market. Picotee ranunculus edged in burgundy add further dimension. White narcissus with orange trumpets provide a happy note. Strands of tuberous nasturtium vines, which are related to the common garden nasturtium, weave through the arrangement.

ALTERNATE FLOWERS In summer, there are roses, marigolds, celosia, and cosmos. In winter, try amaryllis. Warmer, deeper shades appear in fall: rusty dahlias, ginger sunflowers, orange peppers, and persimmons. For accents and added dimension, use burnished leaves and berries.

1 This urn is tall so you don't need to use a frog. Fill three-quarters full with water.

2 Trim the kumquat branches, cutting an X in the bottom of each. Cut away excess foliage. Arrange the branches as the base layer of your arrangement (page 37). Position some of the branches so the kumquats hang over the edge of the urn, with some fruits even dangling toward the table.

3 Trim both types of Parrot tulips to various lengths and add to the urn. Some should stand tall; others should curve outward. Trim and add both types of ranunculus, interspersing them with the tulips.

4 Trim and add the narcissus individually or in groups of three. Trim and seal the poppies by burning the ends (see page 35); they will add a bright note and should be used sparingly. Add the grape hyacinth individually so they poke up like little soldiers.

5 Trim the nasturtium vines and weave each one through the arrangement. Trim the *Clematis montana*. One vine should curve low and touch the table. Another should reach up and halo the entire arrangement.

FOOTED PEWTER URN, MEDIUM

---

7 FRUITED KUMQUAT BRANCHES

7 'AVIGNON' PARROT TULIPS, OR ANOTHER LARGE ORANGE PARROT VARIETY

5 SMALLER ORANGE PARROT TULIPS

3 ORANGE/BURGUNDY PICOTEE RANUNCULUS

5 STANDARD ORANGE RANUNCULUS

12 WHITE NARCISSUS WITH ORANGE TRUMPETS

3 ORANGE ICELAND POPPIES

3 GREEN GRAPE HYACINTH, OR ANY TIPS OF GRAY-GREEN FOLIAGE, LIKE RUSSIAN OLIVE

3 TUBEROUS NASTURTIUM VINES

3 *CLEMATIS MONTANA* VINES

Sunny yellow

Yellow is an optimistic color, filled with light and full of promise. Here's a cheerful trio of small arrangements pairing lemon yellows with hints of white. This is an excellent illustration of the rule of three—grouping three similar vases with related flowers so that the impact is greater than that of any single component. It's important that one vase holds a single type of flower; otherwise, the effect is too busy. Ranunculus anchors this trio. The other vases mix narcissus and ranunculus with a variety of small, white flowers. The key is balance, layering tone on tone, using complementary colors to quiet the brights or highlight the subtler shades. Seeded eucalyptus grows abundantly in some parts of the United States, but it can also be ordered from BunchesDirect.com.

ALTERNATE FLOWERS In summer, use yellow roses and iris; in fall, chrysanthemums and zinnias. In winter, force yellow narcissus. In general, steer clear of classic daffodils because their yellow is so strong it can be overwhelming. However, white narcissus with hints of yellow in the trumpet—or any other bicolor daffodil—works well in a formal or casual arrangement.

FIRST VASE:

WHITE CERAMIC CUP, SMALL

18 YELLOW RANUNCULUS

SECOND VASE:

WHITE CERAMIC MINI COMPOTE, SMALL

3 KOUSA DOGWOOD TIPS

5 YELLOW OR GREEN SEEDED EUCALYPTUS TIPS

12 MINI YELLOW NARCISSUS

5 SPIREA TIPS

THIRD VASE:

WHITE CERAMIC CUP, SMALL

3 FRINGE TREE TIPS

3 YELLOW HYACINTH

25 YELLOW NARCISSUS

5 *CLEMATIS MONTANA* FOLIAGE TIPS

1 Fill the vases three-quarters full with water. Because these are small vases, you need only use the tips of some of the larger branches.

2 For the first vase, pictured on the far right, trim and arrange the ranunculus, alternating buds and open flowers.

3 For the second vase, pictured in the front, trim and anchor the dogwood tips in the vase, with one in the center and the other two to the sides. Trim the eucalyptus and position the tips so they overhang the front of the vase. Trim and add the narcissus in groups of three. Trim and add the spirea tips, making sure that some emerge from the top of the arrangement and others dangle over the edge of the vase.

4 For the third vase, pictured in the back, trim the fringe tree tips and arrange so that they drape over the edge of the vase. Trim and add the hyacinth. Trim and add the narcissus in groups of three or five. Trim the clematis and wind and drape around vase.

PEONY

ICELAND
POPPY

HYDRANGEA

'LA BELLE EPOQUE' TULIP

SWAMP MAPLE

PLUM BRANCHES

Think pink

SWAMP MAPLE
SEED POD

TREE PEONY

Think pink

Pink, the color of grace and elegance, flatters just about everyone, from the pale seashell pink in a little girl's crinoline to the bright pink of a favorite lipstick. Think of the morning sky, with its mauve and salmon, coral and peach—all variations on pink. Here, dark plum foliage adds an edgy contrast to an arrangement of pinks. Since you have so many pinks to choose from, the possible floral combinations are endless: tulips, peonies, lilies, poppies, and more. There's something especially charming about the marriage between peonies and Parrot tulips—ruffle upon ruffle, so feminine and fluffy.

ALTERNATE FLOWERS There is no shortage of pink alternatives: roses, carnations, cymbidium orchids, dianthus, lilies, sweet peas, and snapdragons.

1 Anchor a pin frog at the bottom of the compote with floral putty. Fill three-quarters full with water.

2 Trim the plum and swamp maple branches, and cut an X in the bottom of each. Create a base layer (page 37) by anchoring the plum branches in the center and to the left and right. Add the swamp maple, anchoring some branches so they sweep down over the edge of the compote.

3 Anchor the eucalyptus pods at various angles in the center of the arrangement. Trim the foxgloves and place in the center and at the right and left.

4 Trim both types of tulips and the hydrangeas and peonies. Intersperse them in the arrangement, positioning some upright and letting others hang over the edge of the compote. Make sure you give special prominence to 'La Belle Epoque' tulips, whose coffee-beige blooms are so dramatic.

5 Trim and add the delicate poppies, positioning them at the top. Finish with the clematis vines, trimming them and circling them up and around the arrangement.

PEWTER COMPOTE, MEDIUM

PIN FROG

FLORAL PUTTY

7 PLUM BRANCHES, FOLIAGE ONLY

5 VARIEGATED SWAMP MAPLE BRANCHES

5 BROWN EUCALYPTUS PODS

5 GREEN FOXGLOVES

15 PINK STAR TULIPS

7 BEIGE 'LA BELLE EPOQUE' TULIPS

3 PINK HYDRANGEAS

3 CHERRY PINK TREE PEONIES

3 LIGHT PINK PEONIES

3 PEACH ICELAND POPPIES

5 *CLEMATIS MONTANA* VINES

spring ‖ # Tonal contrast

"So the darkness shall be the light, and the stillness the dancing," wrote poet T. S. Eliot. Contrast can be very effective. Rather than use analogous colors, like pink and orange, try opposites. The key is to keep the color balance simple: a soft color with a stronger one. Here, pale yellows are paired with bold burgundies. The inspiration is the bicolor nasturtium, which beautifully combines both tones. The ranunculus and the orchids have similar contrasting colors.

ALTERNATE FLOWERS In early summer, pair pale pink peonies with plummy oncidium orchids. In fall, purple dahlias with hot pink roses.

1 You don't need to use an anchor with this narrow-necked vase. Fill it three-quarters full with water.

2 Trim the plum branches, and cut an X in the bottom of each. Arrange the branches to form a base layer (page 37) for the flowers and create a halo of burgundy.

3 Trim the cymbidium orchids. Allow them to hang over the edge of the vase and form the bottom edge of the arrangement. Trim the phalaenopsis orchids. They should arc out to either side of the vase, extending the horizontal form of the arrangement.

BLACK CERAMIC VASE, SMALL

4 When trimming the ranunculus, keep them taller than the narcissus. Intersperse throughout the arrangement, making sure they stand taller than the other flowers. Trim the narcissus and add in groups of three and five. They should sit low and fill the center of the arrangement.

5 PLUM BRANCHES, FOLIAGE ONLY

6 BURGUNDY CYMBIDIUM ORCHID STEMS

3 SPOTTED PHALAENOPSIS ORCHID STEMS

7 PLUM-EDGED YELLOW RANUNCULUS

15 MINI YELLOW NARCISSUS

6 PURPLE CHERVIL STEMS

5 CHECKERED LILIES

12 YELLOW AND BURGUNDY NASTURTIUMS

5 Trim the chervil stems. The fringed leaves, resembling ferns, pick up the burgundy color of the orchids and add a feathery touch. Poke them into the arrangement so they fan out, adding height and width, at the top and on both sides.

6 Trim the checkered lilies. Drape them over the front edge of the vase. Trim the nasturtiums, keeping the stems long so they can float over the other flowers. Add to the vase in groups of three.

IVY

CLEMATIS

Blue mood

DELPHINIUM

GENTIAN

DELPHINIUM TIP

Blue mood

Blue is the most difficult color to find in the garden. Shades of purple abound, but true cerulean—the color of Delft porcelain—is a rarity. Yet the blues that nature does deliver are extraordinary. Most notable is the delphinium, its multiflowered spires ranging from soft robin's-egg blue to cobalt and sapphire, sometimes in a single blossom. Because delphiniums are such dramatic, upright flowers, they don't need a large supporting cast. In this arrangement, they float over a cloud of 'Jackmanii' clematis and blue gentians. The drift of clematis adds a fluttering element to the statuesque delphinium spires.

ALTERNATE FLOWERS Delphiniums are unequaled, but many of the best blue flowers blossom early in spring: perky grape hyacinths and light blue forget-me-nots. Pair them with green-and-white tulips, which flower at the same time. In late summer, hydrangeas range from lilac to lavender to green to blue in a single mophead.

1 You don't need to use a frog, as the vase is tall enough to support the flowers. Fill three-quarters full with water.

2 Trim the magnolia branches, cutting an X in the bottom of each. Position the branches so they overhang the vase.

3 Trim the delphiniums. Stand them together in the center of the vase if the arrangement is to be viewed from all sides, or toward the back if the arrangement is to be placed against a wall.

4 Trim the gentians. Add in multiples of three and five between the magnolia branches and the delphiniums. They have stiff stems and will remain rigid.

5 Trim the clematis and intersperse the vines among the gentians. Weave the ivy through the flowers and let some reach down onto the table.

IVORY FOOTED CERAMIC VASE, MEDIUM

10 MAGNOLIA BRANCH TIPS, FOLIAGE ONLY

20 DELPHINIUMS IN VARIOUS SHADES OF BLUE

15 BLUE GENTIANS

5 'JACKMANII' CLEMATIS VINES

5 IVY VINES

Shades of green

Most often, green plays a supporting role in floral design. Green foliage punctuates a bouquet, adding background and subtle shading to the dominant color. Now and then, green steps into the spotlight, as it does in this summery arrangement of green 'Envy' zinnias. The zinnias were an unusual find in nurseries even five years ago, but once discovered by designers and gardeners, they became a regular in the flower garden. The color is delightful, sort of a buttery chartreuse, and when paired with a variety of other shapes and sizes of green blossoms, including the numerous petals of a still-ripening 'Annabelle' hydrangea, the zinnias hit the spot.

ALTERNATE FLOWERS In spring and summer, bells of Ireland, stems of *Hypericum* berries, and green roses. In fall and winter, spider mums, cymbidium orchids, and lime green hydrangeas.

1 You don't need an anchor for this heavy pitcher. Fill three-quarters full with water.

2 Trim the berry branches. Sink them deep into the pitcher so the fruits drip over the lip.

3 Trim the zinnias to a variety of lengths. Add to the pitcher among the berry branches. Trim the hydrangeas, and cut an X in the bottom of each stem. They should be taller than the zinnias. Intersperse throughout the arrangement.

4 Trim the nicotianas. Position some of the blossoms to curve down below the vase and others to rise above the other flowers.

5 Trim the love in a puff. Some vines should curve downward, with puffs touching the table. Others should fly up and away from the arrangement. Trim the ivy and arrange so one piece circles up into the arrangement and the other piece drapes onto the table.

PEWTER PITCHER, MEDIUM

---

6 GREEN VIBURNUM BERRY BRANCHES

10 GREEN 'ENVY' ZINNIAS

8 'ANNABELLE' HYDRANGEAS

10 GREEN NICOTIANAS

5 LOVE IN A PUFF VINES

2 IVY VINES

Certain flowers endlessly fascinate and beguile. How could any of us live without tulips, roses, dahlias, or peonies? More than any other bloom, the tulip takes a beautiful journey, from bud to tight blossom to full-blown flower. It dances and moves with the light; more to the point, it changes color as it matures. Tulips will play tricks on you. Fashion an arrangement in the evening, placing each tulip to its best advantage, and come morning, you'll find them all standing at attention like a battalion of soldiers. That's why they often do best on their own.

No bloom is more popular than a rose, and today's garden roses are miracles of modern breeding. Horticulturalists have taken the best of the old-school roses, their blowsy forms and deep aromas, and married them to the multiple blooming habits of formal tea roses. Their luxurious shape, scent, and abundance add romance and sensuality to any arrangement.

Then there are the dahlias. More sculptural and rigid than roses— growing in seemingly infinite colors, shapes, and sizes atop leafy, thornless stems—dahlias are the foundation of many late-summer arrangements. They are also very easy to grow. Plant a dahlia corm one year, and you'll have double the amount the next. They are a good investment and a great flower.

No list of favorites would be complete without the tree peony. It is the empress of the flower world. You can stare at a single bloom, with its golden stamens and frilly, multihued petals, for an entire day and still not tire of its gradations of color and its perfect structure. "To see a world in a grain of sand, and a heaven in a wild flower," wrote poet William Blake. The tree peony is heaven.

People often ask me what my favorite flower is, and I just laugh. Give me a season, I say, and I'll name three—it's like choosing your favorite child. Tulips, roses, dahlias, and peonies are the well-loved royals of the plant world, and rightfully so. But I have my own, less dramatic favorites that show up again and again in my arrangements, sometimes taking center stage, sometimes playing harmony.

Take the simple carnation. Often dismissed, the once lowly bloom has now been hybridized into a gorgeous array of colors, from burnt red to cocoa, from the palest pink to variegated blooms with dark pink edges. These lovely, long-lasting, no-fuss flowers add dimension to any arrangement.

Kaye Heafey, owner of Chalk Hill Clematis Farm in California, where I've hosted a number of flower workshops, says, "Clematis arrange themselves." I quite agree. These woody, climbing vines are regulars in my arrangements—wrapped around footed vases and woven through branches, mimicking their natural habits. Clematis has been a staple in the English garden for well over a century, and thanks to hybridization, larger, more colorful flowers are now available. But I hold a special place in my heart for sweet autumn clematis (*Clematis paniculata*, aka *C. terniflora*), delicate white blossoms that grow abundantly and dance like feathers in any arrangement.

Hellebores are a once-rare flower that has been hybridized into popularity. The most common have pale green flowers and emerge early in spring, sometimes when the ground is still snow covered. Today, you'll find hellebores in deep burgundy, mauve, or white, or in dappled mixtures of those shades. They seem almost waxlike in their perfection.

Tulip

Tulips are the only flower ever traded as currency. The Dutch were so enamored of them that, in 1634, investors triggered a speculative frenzy known as "tulip mania." Today, the tulip remains a valuable Dutch commodity, with breeders producing three billion bulbs a year, mostly for export.

Tulips come in multiple varieties; more colors and sizes are being hybridized each year. Standard tulips, the ones you most often see in the supermarket, appear in numerous colors. Other variations include the double tulip, which looks like a peony, and the fringed tulip, whose petals appear like the edges of a tassled shawl.

Parrot tulips bloom slightly later than standards and are known for their multihued, flamelike markings. Depending on the variety, their petals can be curled or twisted. They are the drama queens of the genus.

French tulips are among the most breathtaking of the tulip family. The name is something of a misnomer; originally, these tulips might have been hybridized in the south of France, but they are grown most abundantly in the Netherlands. French tulips are larger, and therefore must have longer, thicker stems for support. They bloom later in the spring, and some, like my current favorite, 'Avignon', have been crossbred with Parrots to create remarkable color palettes. 'Avignon' is a huge variety that looks like the sunset, shading from pink to coral to yellow. However, with every trip to the flower shop, you're sure to find other spectacular varieties such as 'Golden Artist', 'Cummins', 'Charming Beauty', and 'La Belle Epoque'.

If you are displaying tulips on their own, as in this arrangement, choose a container that holds the flowers upright but doesn't constrain them. You want them free enough to bend and flow with the day.

FOOTED WHITE CERAMIC VASE, LARGE

---

30 'AVIGNON' PARROT TULIPS

10 FRENCH PEACH TULIPS

10 FRENCH YELLOW-AND-PEACH TULIPS

CONTINUED

Tulip, continued ‖ **1** This is a tall vase, so it does not require a frog. Fill three-quarters full with water.

2 Clip the tulip stems to remove any white at the bottom. Also remove most of the foliage—never leave more than two leaves on any stem, as the leaves compete with the flowers for water. Make sure that the stems are one or two times the height of the vase.

3 Add the 'Avignon' tulips to the vase first, then intersperse the other tulips throughout.

HOW TO MAKE A TULIP "FLOAT"

If you want to add some variety to your tulip arrangements, bend the petals of a half-opened tulip back and open, as if bending back the ribs of a little umbrella. The flower will open up wide and take an altogether different shape.

| # Hellebore

If you like to build tone-on-tone arrangements, the hellebore is a natural ally. This unique flower, an early spring bloomer, arrives with a muted palette that ranges from white to pink to mauve, sometimes all in the same flower. It's such an unusual blossom—with leathery, evergreen foliage—that you can use it as a stand-alone flower, pairing a mix of varieties in simple vases for a table setting that always draws comments. New hybrids appear regularly, featuring double blossoms and dramatic veining. These are easy plants to grow in a shade garden, and they multiply abundantly.

To extend the hellebore's life as a cut flower, dip the stems in hot water after trimming, then let them rest in cold water overnight.

1 The blossoms are small and don't require anchors. Fill the vase three-quarters full with water.

2 Trim the hellebores to varying heights and place six in the vase, interspersing fully opened blossoms with those that are slightly closed.

3 Select two hellebore flowers of different colors, remove the stems, and float each in a shallow dish of water.

GLASS VASE, SMALL

2 SHALLOW DISHES

8 HELLEBORES OF
DIFFERENT VARIETIES

PHALAENOPSIS
ORCHID

Peony

HELLEBORE

PEONY

PURPLE CHERVIL

RANUNCULUS

Peony

Peonies are generous flowers. These fluffy, long-lasting blooms blossom
in a range of colors—from bright white to yellow, coral, and peach, to
pink and red. Tree peonies, which grow as a woody shrub, can contain
a variety of shades in a single blossom. When they're in season, in
May and June, they make a spectacular addition to bridal bouquets, as
they are the very definition of romance. Herbaceous peonies die back
to the ground each year and are born on new, green stems. They are
especially varied, coming in single, double, and multipetaled versions
that are so huge they are called "bombs." Peonies are also well-behaved
blossoms, easily trimmed and, like tulips, fun to watch as their petals
open and progress through a long life cycle.

ALTERNATE FLOWERS To complement the peonies, use any of
the many white viburnums that blossom at the same time, white
narcissus, or late tulips.

1 Fasten a flower frog to the bottom of the vase with floral putty. Fill
three-quarters full with water.

2 Trim the spirea branches, cutting an X in the bottom of each. Add to
the vase to form a base layer (page 37) for the arrangement. Trim the
dogwood branches 2 inches shorter than the spirea, cutting an X in
the bottom of each. Position them next to the spirea.

3 Trim the peonies and place in the vase. Three should be cut to arch
over the edge of the vase. The rest can be 1 or 2 inches longer so they
have more height.

4 Trim the ranunculus and add in bunches of two or three, interspersing
them between the peonies and the dogwood. Trim the orchids and add
so they arch beyond the arrangement—two out of the top, the others
out either side. Trim and add the hellebores to nestle between the other
blossoms.

5 Trim the jasmine and tuck short stems into the vase so the flowers
extend below the edge. Trim the chervil. Some stems should be positioned
at the top of the arrangement. Others should arch downward, toward
the table.

FOOTED WHITE VASE, MEDIUM

PIN FROG

FLORAL PUTTY

---

5 SPIREA BRANCHES

4 KOUSA DOGWOOD BRANCHES

8 PINK 'MRS. FRANKLIN D.
ROOSEVELT' PEONIES

6 WHITE RANUNCULUS

4 BLUSH PHALAENOPSIS
ORCHID STEMS

5 HELLEBORES

5 JASMINE VINES

5 PURPLE CHERVIL STEMS

Clematis

Though you may be most familiar with the purple-and-blue 'Jackmanii' clematis, which has long been popular in the United States, there are three hundred species of clematis in an array of shapes, colors, and sizes. Each would add charm and a bit of whimsy to any arrangement. In this simple bouquet, clematis vines in a trio of related tones contrast with an elegant sliver pitcher. Every element adds to the overall effect: acrobatic leaves, tight buds, and starbursts of color. Clematis is a staple of the flower market, but is also easy to grow.

1 You do not need an anchor for this narrow-necked pitcher. Fill three-quarters full with water.

2 Trim the clematis stems. They are too small to cut an X in the bottom, so instead crush them so they absorb water well.

3 Arrange the stems by color, shading from dark to light. Don't overcrowd the pitcher. It's best to accentuate the airy, floating quality of the clematis vines by leaving adequate space.

FOOTED SILVER PITCHER WITH
NARROW NECK, SMALL

12 CLEMATIS VINES IN THREE
SHADES OF BLUE OR VIOLET

Garden rose

The classic long-stemmed red rose is the Red Delicious apple of the flower world. But there is something far more lovely about the old-fashioned garden rose, its soft petals inviting you to breathe in its scent. These are the roses you may have discovered in your grandmother's garden, and they are back again in a variety of soft shades.

Historically, the garden rose did not have a long shelf life. Standards like the magnificent, pure pink Constance Spry rose, deep cupped and delicate, bloomed only once in early summer. But it was this blossom that inspired English rose breeder David Austin to revolutionize the rose industry. In the early 1960s, he crossed old roses with hybrid tea roses and floribundas to create a modern English rose with sturdier, longer-lasting blossoms that held their scent and bloomed more than once a season.

One of the first roses to make this transition was 'Juliet', a glorious apricot-peach blossom. Now you will find many competing beauties, such as the 'Abraham Darby', the 'Eglantyne', and the 'Distant Drums' used in this arrangement.

ALTERNATE FLOWERS Any similar shade of fruiting branch can replace the apricots, such as crabapples or peaches. You can substitute jasmine for the clematis.

1 Because the vase is tall, you don't need to use a frog. Fill three-quarters full with water.

2 Trim the apricot branches, and cut an X in the bottom of each. Arrange in the vase so the apricots hang over the edge.

3 Trim the roses. Alternate fully open blossoms with smaller blooms in different stages of budding. Though they are all the same type of rose, each blossom looks unique.

4 Trim the eucalyptus and add at the base of the arrangement so the pods reach below the edge of the vase.

5 Trim the clematis vines. Weave them through the arrangement, making sure that the wisps of the flowers and leaves create a halo over the entire bouquet.

GRAY-GREEN CYLINDRICAL
CERAMIC VASE, TALL

5 FRUITED APRICOT BRANCHES

20 'DISTANT DRUMS' ROSES

5 EUCALYPTUS POD STEMS

5 SWEET AUTUMN CLEMATIS VINES

Dahlia

In autumn, shrubs harvested in spring for their blossoms deliver a different kind of beauty: leaves ranging from red-brown to purple to rusty orange. They find no better companions than a host of giant dahlias in sunset colors. Dahlias start blooming in late July and can be harvested through October if the frost doesn't bite. They come in a variety of sizes and are easy to grow in the garden. Autumn also offers unusual flowers, none more interesting than the prehistoric-looking spiky blooms of the castor bean. Dogwood produces green-going-to-red fruits, and Russian olive delivers delightful red berries. Last but not least, the pods of the love in a puff vine, resembling little chartreuse lanterns, float throughout the arrangement.

ALTERNATE FLOWERS In summer, use peonies or roses instead of dahlias, proteas or pink alliums instead of castor flowers, copper beech branches, and sweet pea vines to replace love in a puff.

CERAMIC COMPOTE, LARGE

WATERPROOF CONTAINER

PIN FROG

FLORAL PUTTY

NEWSPAPER

MOSS

1 If your ceramic compote is porous and cannot hold water, like the one used here, place a waterproof container inside. Anchor a pin frog in the container with floral putty. Fill three-quarters full with water. Add balled-up newspaper around the container to hold it steady and cover the newspaper with moss.

5 OAKLEAF HYDRANGEA BRANCHES

6 CASTOR BEAN FLOWERS

5 DOGWOOD BRANCHES WITH FALL FRUITS

5 MAROON VIBURNUM BRANCHES

10 FRUITED RUSSIAN OLIVE BRANCHES

4 SWEET AUTUMN CLEMATIS VINES

4 LOVE IN A PUFF VINES

10 LARGE SALMON DAHLIAS

8 GIANT PEACH DAHLIAS

10 PINK DAHLIAS

2 Trim the hydrangea branches, and cut an X in the bottom of each. Anchor them so they extend horizontally over the edge of the compote. Trim the castor flowers and add next to the hydrangea, repeating the horizontal placement.

3 Trim the dogwood and viburnum branches, and cut an X in the bottom of each. Place them so they arch out either side of the arrangement, creating a horizontal structure. Trim and add 8 olive branches, turning some so the backs of the leaves show. All of these branches act as a base layer (page 37) for the flowers.

CONTINUED

4 Trim and anchor the clematis vines to the frog. Wind them through the branches and circle them below the compote. Trim the love in a puff vines. Anchor them to the frog and wind them through the branches, and arch them down in front of the compote so the green "puffs" dangle from the arrangement.

5 Trim all the dahlias and remove most of the leaves. Some of the blossoms should sit "low" in the compote. These can be cut as short as 3 to 4 inches. Some dahlias should be anchored to overhang the edge of the compote. Use dahlias with longer stems to fill the center of the compote.

6 Trim fruit from remaining branches of Russian olive and intersperse among dahlias.

‖ Dahlia, continued

Carnation

A stalwart frill of a flower, the carnation has long been dismissed as a "buttonhole" bloom, whose purpose is to lounge on a man's lapel. Dipped in green dye and sold in supermarket bunches for St. Patrick's Day, carnations are often seen as common blossoms, unworthy of being a star attraction. But just like the English garden rose, the carnation has benefited from hybridization. Today, carnations come in more than two hundred shades, from frilly whites to dramatic burgundies, from deep purples to soft pinks. The carnation is an obvious addition to tonal arrangements, especially since so many of them are bred as bicolor blossoms that can fit in with multiple color themes.

ALTERNATE FLOWERS Since carnations are the focal flower here, avoid adding any larger, overly dramatic supporting flowers. Instead, use small dahlias, stock, sweet peas, or anemones.

1 Because the vases have narrow necks, you don't need an anchor. Fill each three-quarters full with water.

2 For the small vase, select 10 to 12 carnations of varying shades. Trim the stems, cutting them to the length of the vase so the carnations rest on the lip.

3 For the second vase, trim the remaining carnations and add in groups of three or five, pairing colors in a variety of ways.

4 Trim the lilies and add to the larger vase, beneath the carnations, so they drape over the edge of the vase.

5 Trim the abutilon. Add to the larger vase singly and in groups of three. Trim and add the hellebores to the larger vase, interspersing them with other flowers.

6 Trim the passion flower vines. Wind them into and above the larger arrangement.

2 FOOTED PEWTER VASES, 1 SMALL AND 1 MEDIUM

5 TO 6 EACH OF 6 CARNATION VARIETIES: BEIGE, PALE PINK, MAUVE, WHITE, RASPBERRY, LILAC

6 WHITE *NERINE* LILIES

12 PINK ABUTILONS

6 PURPLE HELLEBORES

3 GREEN PASSION FLOWER VINES

Branch
arrangements

Branches are the architecture of any arrangement, providing structure, height, grace, and balance. You can use branches on their own when you want to make a big impression in a large space—a church nave, for example, or a high-ceilinged room. Their impact can be so dramatic that the space requires nothing more.

Arboreal possibilities are limitless, depending on the season. Throughout the year, the copper beech, with its deep burgundy leaves, is particularly grand, while the delicate weeping willow provides curves and wisp. For fall, search out branches of winged euonymus, which turns red in autumn, or forsythia, whose leaves turn a dark maroon. Viburnum leaves become purple and often have upright berries. In the winter, delight in the stark beauty of white pine. Flowering trees and shrubs offer their own springtime rewards: crabapple or plum blossoms, decorative quince, dogwood, lilac, and magnolia. In the summer, seek out apricots, peaches, and other fruited branches (see Fruits and Berries chapter, page 133).

Preparation is crucial when adding branches to any arrangement. You must cut or smash the woody stems so they will take in sufficient water. Whenever possible, I recommend using a double cut, in the form of an X, at the base of each stem, since smashing will often cause the branches to cloud the water in a glass vase. If a branch is thin, a single cut will suffice.

Choose some branches for their leaves—like the dependable copper beech—and some for their architecture. Be sure to strip the latter of foliage so the wood is revealed. For some branches, you can pull away the leaves to reveal seedpods, as with ash or linden; for other arrangements, you want only branches with blossoms.

Branches are often the starting point for an arrangement, their woody stems creating a superstructure upon which to build. If your vase is tall enough, a floral frog won't be necessary, but it's always a good idea to make sure that large urns are heavy enough so your arrangement won't take a tumble.

HOW TO EDIT A BRANCH ARRANGEMENT

The beauty of a branch lies in its architecture, and the art of revealing this architecture often requires editing.

Select branches that arch in a variety of directions. These will form your base layer (page 37). It's easier to work with branches that already lean in one direction or another.

• Using pruning shears or scissors, trim the leaves on each bough to expose the structure of the branch. If using a fruited bough, for example, the goal is to reveal the fruit. Therefore, you should trim off any leaves that get in the way. Sometimes, you want to show only the fruit, especially with a particularly exotic, gnarly branch. Other times, you want to keep some leaves if they add to the overall look of the arrangement. If using a branch for its colorful leaves, simply thin the leaves so the best ones stand out. If your goal is to reveal only seedpods, then all leaves must go.

• Trim off any dead or discolored twigs, foliage, or fruit.

• Trim the bottom of the branches, and cut an X in the bottom of each stem so it can better absorb water. Remove all leaves that will fall below the waterline.

• Anchor the branches with a floral frog, if necessary. You do not need an anchor if the vase is deep or its opening is narrow. Stand back and look at the branches in the vase. The leaves should not overlap or crowd the vase and should not sit below the water level. You may want to edit further.

Flowering dogwood

When everyone in the photo studio saw the branches of this flowering dogwood, they gasped. The dogwood was at its peak of bloom—which lasts for days—and the flowers looked like little petticoats all aflutter. Here's an instance when nature is so generous, and so beautiful, that all you have to do is let it be. Just clip away any dead branches so the flower drifts stand out. Using a glass vase makes the cloud of petals appear weightless.

ALTERNATE FLOWERS Any blooming branch will do, though dogwood is especially delicate. Try flowering quince, plum, or pear.

1 The vase is large, so you do not need to use an anchor. Fill three-quarters full with water.

2 Trim each branch, and cut an X in the bottom of each. Position the branches in the center and arching to the right and left. The goal is to create a flat, horizontal plane, as the branches will rest in front of a wall. If you like, trim and position a smaller branch so the flowers float below the vase.

TALL, FOOTED GLASS VASE, LARGE

5 KOUSA DOGWOOD BRANCHES

Crabapple blossoms

Crabapple trees are so versatile. They are drought tolerant, so you'll find they are as popular in Colorado as in New England. These easy-to-grow small trees flower in pink and white, with single or double blossoms. Better still, many have showy fall leaves, from yellow to orange to red and purple. What more could you ask for in a tree? Here, pink crabapple flowers are combined with white hawthorn branches. The surprise is a base of olive branches anchored to dip down over the urn, their gray-green leaves contrasting with the bright flowers. To finish this arrangement, add a variety of spring blossoms in shades of pink and white.

ALTERNATE FLOWERS Replace the crabapples with pear or apple blossoms or mock orange (*Philadelphus*). Other flower options: white narcissus, white or pink peonies.

1 The urn is deep enough that it does not require an anchor. Fill three-quarters full with water.

2 Trim the crabapple branches, and cut an X in the bottom of each. Position the branches to form a base layer (page 37), placing them in the center of the urn and arching to the right and left.

3 Trim the hawthorn branches, and cut an X in the bottom of each. Intersperse the branches among the crabapple. They will form a fanlike backdrop for the flowers.

4 Trim the foxgloves to three-quarters of the height of the tallest branches. These will provide a medium-range focus for the arrangement. Position some extending up into the center of the arrangement and others overlapping the edge of the urn and extending downward.

5 Trim the olive branches, and cut an X in the bottom of each. Add them to the urn so they curve down over the edge of the urn on the left and right sides.

6 Trim the carnations, anemones, and ranunculus so they occupy the lower third of the arrangement, and position them in the center of the urn.

WHITE, FOOTED URN, MEDIUM

---

3 TO 5 CRABAPPLE BRANCHES WITH PINK BLOSSOMS

3 OR 4 WHITE HAWTHORN BRANCHES

6 WHITE FOXGLOVE STEMS

5 PINK FOXGLOVE STEMS

5 OLIVE BRANCHES

10 PINK CARNATIONS

5 WHITE ANEMONES

3 RED-AND-WHITE RANUNCULUS

White branch arrangement

Branch arrangements are the easiest way to fill a room with flowers, and this abundant display presents both single and double blossoms of one species—mock orange (*Philadelphus*). Single-blossom mock orange is a common variety and can be found growing in country gardens all over the United States; the hybrid double blossom has more petals in the flower (if you can't locate double-blossom mock orange, you can use just the single-blossom variety). If set against a white wall, the arching branches need no augmentation. The drama is in the placement of the branches, which should arch as if still on the bush.

ALTERNATE FLOWERS White lilacs, apple or pear blossoms, dogwood, or viburnum, or any nicely arching shrub at its peak of bloom.

1 Anchor a large yogurt container to the bottom of the urn with floral putty. Fill three-quarters full with water. Wedge balled-up newspapers around the plastic container for stability.

2 Trim the mock orange branches, and cut an X in the bottom of each. Strip away any lower leaves that will be below the water level. Position the branches in as natural an arch as possible, with some in the center of the vase and others arching to the right and left. Note how the double blossoms arch through the center of the arrangement, balancing the airiness of the branches with single blossoms.

CAST IRON URN, LARGE

LARGE YOGURT CONTAINER

FLORAL PUTTY

NEWSPAPERS

15 MOCK ORANGE (*PHILADELPHUS*) BRANCHES, HALF DOUBLE FLOWERED, HALF SINGLE FLOWERED

Branches in white and green

Sometimes it's fun to surprise your visitors with an unexpected guest. The same is true for this flower arrangement, which invites a vegetable garden staple into the mix. This "dangle" of sugar snap peas reminds us that there is no limit to the greenery that can find its way into a flower arrangement. You can use fruit, nuts, grasses—whatever works. Much of this late-spring arrangement can be harvested from a backyard garden or may be discovered at a local farmers' market.

White and green, in all its many shades, are two of the first colors to break the long winter cycle, and they always look good together. The 'Tardiva' hydrangeas in this arrangement are weeks from blooming into full white blossoms, but this early, green stage can be more interesting.

ALTERNATE FLOWERS Replace the peonies with roses or lilies, the mock orange with white viburnum. Don't fret if you are unable to find a specific flower or vine. The goal is an abundance of green and white, which gives you terrific latitude.

1 Anchor a large yogurt container to the bottom of the urn with floral putty. Fill three-quarters full with water. Wedge balled-up newspapers around the container for stability.

2 Strip the leaves from the linden branches so only the pods remain. Trim the branches, and cut an X in the bottom of each. Do the same with the mock orange. Alternate linden branches with mock orange as the base layer, (page 37) positioning some in the center and others to the left and right.

3 Trim the wisteria. Wrap some about the base of the urn, and the rest through the branches.

4 Trim the peonies to varying lengths and place throughout the arrangement. Do the same with the hydrangeas and lilacs, whose small flowers become a foil for the larger peonies. Trim the Solomon's seal and the lilies. Place throughout the arrangement.

5 Trim the pea vines. Wind them through the arrangement and around the urn, letting the pods dangle around the base.

CERAMIC URN, LARGE

LARGE YOGURT CONTAINER

FLORAL PUTTY

NEWSPAPERS

---

10 LINDEN BRANCHES

3 MOCK ORANGE
(*PHILADELPHUS*) BRANCHES

4 WISTERIA VINES, FOLIAGE ONLY

10 'FESTIVA MAXIMA' PEONIES

5 'TARDIVA' HYDRANGEAS, BEFORE
WHITE MOPHEADS BLOOM

6 WHITE LILAC STEMS

8 VARIEGATED SOLOMON'S
SEAL STEMS

10 *EUCHARIS* LILIES

6 SUGAR SNAP PEA VINES

SNOWBERRY
STEMS

CASTOR BEAN
FLOWERS

WINGED
EUONYMUS

VIBURNUM

Burning branch
arrangement in
shades of pink

JAPANESE
ANEMONES

DAHLIA

LOVE IN A PUFF VINES

‖ # Burning branch arrangement in shades of pink

During fall in the Northeast, the woods are ablaze in sharp oranges, fiery reds, and shimmering yellows. The colors deepen from week to week. But it's not the show-stopping brilliance of the sugar maple that makes this arrangement so spectacular; it's winged euonymus, also known as burning bush, whose leaves change from green to copper to red on a single branch. In New England, the shrub is easy to spot along the roadside or in a neighbor's backyard, but it's invasive so I don't encourage planting it yourself. Various fall blossoms complement the sunset colors, most notably dahlias and also the spiky castor flower, which contrasts so well with delicate pink anemones. All are tied together with the playful green pods of love in a puff.

ALTERNATE FLOWERS Any leaf in color might work in this autumnal arrangement: forsythia, maple, or dogwood. As an alternative to love in a puff, look for grapevines still bearing fruit.

NARROW, FOOTED VASE IN FLAT
BLACK, LARGE

---

8 WINGED EUONYMUS BRANCHES

5 CRANBERRY VIBURNUM
BRANCHES, OR ANY LEAVES OF A
SIMILAR BURGUNDY HUE

6 PINK SNOWBERRY STEMS

5 GIANT RED CACTUS DAHLIAS

20 PINK DAHLIAS

5 RED-AND-WHITE DAHLIAS

5 CASTOR BEAN FLOWERS

20 PINK JAPANESE ANEMONES

3 LOVE IN A PUFF VINES

1 This vase is tall enough that it doesn't need a floral frog. Fill three-quarters full with water.

2 Trim the winged euonymus branches, and cut an X in the bottom of each. Add to the back of the vase to form the base layer (page 37), positioning some in the center and others to the left and right. Trim the viburnum branches, and cut an X in the bottom of each. Arrange among the euonymus. The two varieties will form a backdrop.

3 Trim the snowberries. Place them so they hang over the edge of the vase. Trim the cactus dahlias and position them next to the snowberries and side by side. You want them to make a strong impression. Allow one dahlia to hug the edge of the vase.

4 Trim the remaining dahlias to varying lengths and build an arc of flowers in front of the branches in the background. Trim the castor bean flowers and arrange toward the back. Trim the leggy anemones and intersperse them among the dahlias, positioning them high.

5 Trim the love in a puff vines. Wrap them around and through the arrangement, draping some below the other flowers.

Fruits and berries

It's only natural to include the lushness of ripening fruits in floral displays, since they add interest and texture. A bounty of purple grapes, black cherries, green figs, or yellow plums in an arrangement draws the eye. This was the genius of seventeenth-century Dutch masters whose still lifes with fruits, flowers, and even a few insects so completely captured a fleeting moment in time.

The aim of the arrangements in this chapter is to re-create those moments using fruits that match the season. In winter, try citrus (oranges, lemons, and limes), or perhaps pomegranates and quince. For fall, use crabapples, persimmons, figs, and plums. In summer, forage for blackberry branches, which grow wild along country roads. You might also search out more exotic species, like the hairy fruits of the horse chestnut or purple-red eucalyptus berries.

Whatever your choices, the methods are the same: use fruits that are still on the branch, not artificially wired into an arrangement. Once plucked of their wilting leaves, the branches provide their own clean geometry, adding another level of drama to whatever flowers fill out a design.

Early summer is the best time for using fruited branches, since the fruits are small, firm, and securely attached to the branch. Colors can run the rainbow from green to red to purple on a single bough. Best of all, branches have staying power. A twig filled with figs, or unripe peaches or pears, can last as long as three weeks in water.

Yellow fruit and flower table

Sometimes cut flowers make the best impression when they are paired with other partners. Fruit is a natural colleague: luscious, appetizing, and artful when it shares the same color palette as the flowers. But why stop there? A potted plant, especially one as exotic as these phalaenopsis orchids, takes this table setting to even greater heights. The partnership of yellow and green in the flowers, repeated in the figs and pears, is as comfortable as a summer's day.

ALTERNATE FLOWERS This arrangement would work just as well in shades of peach or pink and apricot. Use tulips and roses, apricots and peaches as the fruit, and freesias or bird of paradise as the potted plant.

GLASS COMPOTE, SMALL

PIN FROG

FLORAL PUTTY

BLACK BOWL, SMALL

PEWTER CACHEPOT, MEDIUM

---

13 GREEN FIGS ON THE STEM

3 WHITE *PIERIS JAPONICA* TIPS

5 VARIEGATED SWAMP
MAPLE BRANCH TIPS

15 ACID YELLOW-GREEN
RANUNCULUS

5 *FRITILLARIA ACMOPETALA*

5 SCENTED GERANIUM TIPS

2 PEARS

CHARTREUSE PHALAENOPSIS
ORCHID PLANT

1 Anchor a pin frog at the bottom of the compote with floral putty. Fill three-quarters full with water.

2 Trim five of the fig stems, and cut an X in the bottom of each. Anchor them so the figs hang over the edge of the compote. Do the same with the *Pieris japonica.*

3 Trim the swamp maple branches, cutting some short so they hang over the edge of the compote and leaving others long to hold positions at the top, right, and left.

4 Trim ranunculus to various lengths, and alternate them with the swamp maple branches. Trim the *Fritillaria acmopetala* and scented geranium tips, and intersperse them among the other flowers.

5 Put the pears and the remaining figs in the black bowl and the orchid in the pewter pot. Group together with the flower arrangement.

Summer fruits

In this arrangement, fruits display a continuum of color from the peachy oranges of the plums, peaches, and apricots to the red-purple of the berries—all acting as a foil for strategically placed roses. The tall glass pitcher lifts the arrangement, as if the roses were ballerinas suspended in space. 'Graham Thomas' roses are the stars, their fulsome, blowsy openness hovering atop the luscious fruit.

ALTERNATE FLOWERS Make sure the flowers you select bloom at the same time as the fruits appear on the branches. Dahlias are a good alternative. You don't need to limit yourself to yellow. Try bolder peaches or soft pinks.

1 The narrow pitcher constricts the long branches, so you don't need a floral frog. Fill three-quarters full with water.

2 Begin with the heaviest and fullest fruiting branches, in this case the plums, followed by the peaches and apricots. Trim the plum branches, and cut an X in the bottom of each. Do the same for the peach and apricot branches. Add the branches to the center of the vase and to the right and left. Because you want to create an arch upon which the roses will float, make sure some of the branches curve toward the table.

3 Trim the blackberry vines and raspberry canes. Position them so they rise above the fruits. Trim the roses. Arrange them side by side in an ascending line above the fruits.

4 Trim the clematis vines. Intersperse them throughout the arrangement so the airy blossoms flutter above the fruits and reach out either side and down to the table.

POSITIONING FRUIT

Here's a quick way to place an additional plum or apricot exactly where you want it. If you push a single piece of fruit deep within the arrangement, it will fill the space, and no one will suspect it was put there after the fact and is not attached to one of the branches. You can also scatter a few loose fruits on the table around the base of the container. Or, as shown here, pair the arrangement with an old-fashioned wooden box filled with fruit, suggesting that you've just returned from picking the fruit at an orchard.

TALL, NARROW GLASS PITCHER, MEDIUM

5 SMALL WILD PLUM BRANCHES

3 PEACH BRANCHES

3 APRICOT BRANCHES

8 THORNLESS BLACKBERRY VINES

6 RASPBERRIES CANES

5 YELLOW 'GRAHAM THOMAS' ROSES

4 SWEET AUTUMN CLEMATIS VINES

Blueberries and blush roses

Here's a sweet arrangement that pairs blush roses with branches of still-ripening blueberries. The green-turning-purple berries are nature's color wheel and a good example of displaying fruit to its best advantage. Because the blueberries are still green, few will be shaken off. You want the berries to stand out, so it's best to remove all the leaves from the branches. Classic sweet peas contrast with the blueberries and soften the roses.

For small bouquets, use a fluted vase. The ice-cream-cone shape holds the blossoms solidly in place but is wide enough at the top to let the flowers and foliage drape naturally. In the case of the vase pictured here, the berries' round shape is echoed in the vase's bubble pattern.

ALTERNATE FLOWERS Peonies or ranunculus could replace the roses; ripening raspberries or blackberries, the fruit.

1 This vase does not require an anchor. Fill three-quarters full with water.

2 Remove the leaves from the blueberry branches. Place a few of the longer branches in the center of the vase and to the right and left.

3 Trim the roses. Place two or three deep into the arrangement and hanging over the edge of the vase. Position the others individually.

4 Trim the sweet peas. Add the vines so the flowers float above the roses. Trim the ivy. Wind the vines below and above the flowers.

5 Fill any remaining spaces with the smaller blueberry branches and azalea branch tips.

FLUTED, HOBNAIL GLASS VASE, SMALL

---

8 BLUEBERRY BRANCHES

12 CHAMPAGNE ROSES

15 SWEET PEA VINES, WHITE WITH PURPLE EDGES

2 IVY VINES

5 AZALEA BRANCH TIPS

Yellow roses, crabapples, and quince

Early fall is a cornucopia, a time when everything in nature is ripe and ready for picking. This arrangement was inspired by a farmer's harvest of quince and crabapples. Quince are an heirloom fruit that brings a lovely lumpy-bumpy quality to the arrangement. Color is the unifying theme for this arrangement. Using the yellow-green of the quince and the rust-yellow of the crabapples for inspiration, you can choose any flower in a similar shade and build upon that theme. Dahlias are abundant at this time and available in so many shades.

ALTERNATE FLOWERS Replace the quince with pears, the crabapples with rose hips. You could use giant dahlias instead of roses. In spring, select peonies.

1 Because the vase is so tall, no anchor is required. Fill three-quarters full with water.

2 Remove most of the leaves from the crabapple branches so the fruit is revealed. Remove all leaves from the quince branches. Trim the branches, and cut an X in the bottom of each. Cut the quince branches short enough to hang over the edge of the vase. Position the crabapple branches so some stand upright and others bend to the left or right.

3 Remove the leaves from the olive branches so only the fruits remain. Trim the branches, and cut an X in the bottom of each. Intersperse them with the crabapple branches.

4 Trim the roses to varying lengths so that they sit from 10 to 14 inches above the edge of the vase. Trim the dahlias, lilies, anemones, and carnations. Position one or two roses near the center of the arrangement. Place the other roses individually, alternating them with the dahlias, lilies, anemones, and carnations.

5 Trim the vines, and weave them through, up, and around the arrangement.

TALL BLUE GLASS VASE, LARGE

---

8 CRABAPPLE BRANCHES

4 GREEN QUINCE BRANCHES

6 FRUITED RUSSIAN OLIVE BRANCHES

10 'GRAHAM THOMAS' ROSES

8 'APPLEBLOSSOM' DAHLIAS

8 CAFÉ AU LAIT DAHLIAS

8 YELLOW GLORIOSA LILIES

10 WHITE JAPANESE ANEMONES

5 PUTUMAYO CARNATIONS

5 *STEPHANANDRA INCISA* VINES, OR ANY IVY

Fruits and berries   141

fall ‖ # Dahlias and grapes

Wild grapevines, the inspiration for this arrangement, are complemented by spectacular burgundy dahlias and small zinnias in similar tones. You could set a simple bowl of deep purple plums next to the arrangement to echo its colors and further enhance the autumnal setting. Dahlias and zinnias are both easy to grow. Dahlia corms can be planted in the early spring and will produce flowers well into the fall. They can even be lifted, stored, and reused the next season. Zinnia seedlings are often sold in six-packs at local farmers' markets. If you can't find Persian carpet zinnias, you can plant them yourself from seed. The gold vase, which is wider at the top than the bottom, makes this arrangement supremely graceful and elegant.

ALTERNATE FLOWERS Replace the dahlias with roses or ranunculus. Use blueberry branches instead of grapevines.

1 This vase is deep enough not to need an anchor. Fill three-quarters full with water.

2 Remove the leaves from two grapevines, cut them short, and position the grapes in the vase so they hang over the edge.

3 Trim the burgundy dahlias. Make sure that at least three hang over the edge of the vase. Trim the two-tone burgundy dahlias. Alternate the remaining burgundy dahlias with the two-tone dahlias.

GOLD HEXAGONAL VASE, MEDIUM

4 Trim the roses and place them toward the center of the arrangement. Trim the zinnias, leaving them long enough so they sit above the other flowers in the vase.

5 Trim the remaining grapevine, leaving the grapes, and place toward the back of the arrangement.

3 WILD GRAPEVINES WITH FRUIT

10 BURGUNDY DAHLIAS

6 Wrap the whole arrangement, high and low, with the ivy.

10 TWO-TONE BURGUNDY DAHLIAS

5 'DARCEY' ROSES

12 PERSIAN CARPET ZINNIAS

2 *STEPHANANDRA INCISA* VINES,
OR ANY IVY

Citrus wreath

A square wreath is a refreshing change from the traditional round one. The foundation of this wreath is bay laurel, which is then decorated with citrus. Not only does bay laurel smell good, but if you choose pesticide-free culinary bay, you can pick the leaves off the wreath for cooking. The lemons pictured here are pink-and-yellow-striped calamansi, but any small lemon variety will work. Citrus are easy to wire, as are the branches. Wreaths also make lovely table centerpieces, especially when a candle is placed in the center.

ALTERNATE FLOWERS Use persimmons or pears in place of the lemons.

1 Prepare the fruits. Select eighteen kumquats, and pierce each like a lollipop with a piece of wooden skewer; do not push the skewer all the way through the kumquat. For any remaining fruits that have stems, wrap stem wire around the stems of the fruits, leaving extra wire hanging off to attach to the wreath. For fruits lacking stems, pierce the rind with stem wire and feed the wire through so that it comes out on the same side of the fruit (see photo, page 144). Twist the two ends of the wire together to form a single wire "tail."

2 Cut the bay branches and privet branches to lengths measuring 3 to 5 inches. Make sure the bay branches consist mostly of leaves, not just stems.

3 Stack three bay and three privet berry branches on top of each another, slightly staggered, and secure them with paddle wire into a bunch. Repeat until you have ten bunches. Attach a wired fruit to the base of each bunch, alternating among oranges, tangerines, lemons, and kumquats.

4 Lay the ten bunches on top of the frame, concentrating them in two opposite corners of the wreath. Attach them to the frame with paddle wire.

5 Stack three of the remaining bay branches, one on top of another, so they are slightly staggered. Secure them with paddle wire, lay them on top of the frame in between the two fruited corners, and then wrap paddle wire around the frame. Continue stacking and wiring the bay branches in groups of three until you have covered the frame.

6 Wire any remaining fruits onto the corners of the frame, sinking them deep into the bay leaves. Insert the remaining skewered kumquats in groups of three to the same corners to finish.

CONTINUED

23 FLORAL STEM WIRES, 18 GAUGE

6 WOODEN SKEWERS, CUT INTO 3-INCH PIECES

PADDLE WIRE, 20 GAUGE

12-INCH-SQUARE WIRE WREATH FRAME

---

30 KUMQUATS

2 SMALL BLOOD ORANGES

2 TANGERINES

7 VARIEGATED OR YELLOW LEMONS

25 BAY LAUREL BRANCHES

20 PRIVET BRANCHES WITH BERRIES

A fruited wreath, charmingly square, uses bay laurel as its base, which means you can pluck a leaf and use it for cooking dinner.

Handheld bouquets

All of the bouquets in this chapter, whether they are for a bride or a favorite friend, reflect the practice of building flowers tone on tone. One bouquet may range from yellow to peach to pink; another will wander through pink to purple to burgundy. Some will be primarily white, but with subtle color gradations nonetheless. Carnations make a well-deserved comeback as boutonnieres, in sophisticated new shades and colors.

Once you select your tonal focus, look for a variety of flower shapes that echo that color. Always choose a dramatic focal flower—orchids, tree peonies, a special rose. Next, add smaller, trumpetlike flowers—nicotiana, freesia, lilies. Finally, add floaters, those wispy little flowers that stand out above all the rest—sweet peas, clematis, nasturtiums.

Not all bouquets need to be elaborate. You can make smaller handheld arrangements using just a single flower variety, always looking to the season for inspiration. In May, pick lilies of the valley; in June, ranunculus or roses; in fall, dahlias; and in winter, amaryllis or orchids.

It's always special to grow your own flowers for a wedding bouquet, but you'll have more choice and less anxiety if you contact a flower farmer through your local farmers' market. If you make the connection before the growing season starts, you may be able to request specific varieties of your favorite flowers. For a wedding, the bouquet is the last arrangement you should create, guaranteeing that it is as fresh as possible for the ceremony. You may keep it in water and refrigerate it up to 24 hours before the event

HOW TO MAKE A CASCADING BRIDAL BOUQUET

Building a bouquet is like painting a canvas, layering one color upon another, making sure they are within the same tonal range. When it comes to creating bridal bouquets, every bouquet should be unique, even as it matches the mood of the ceremony and the style of the bride's dress. Always consult with the bride about her chosen colors, bridesmaids' dresses, and favorite flowers, but let what's freshest in the flower market or in the field guide what you include in any arrangement.

When creating a bridal bouquet, stand facing a mirror so you can see how the bouquet will look when it is carried down the aisle.

1 Build from the bottom up, holding all the materials gently in one hand and adding flowers individually with the other hand.

2 Begin with the greens, branches, and vines; seek out elements that are already arching downward.

3 Next, layer the flowers on top of the greens, trimming base flowers long, then adding shorter and shorter stems. Make sure to alternate fuller blossoms with leggier ones.

4 Be patient. (Bridal bouquets can take longer than anything!)

5 Once you've collected more stems than you can hold, fasten them with a rubber band and keep working. You can continue adding stems and foliage, using more rubber bands to contain the blossoms as you proceed.

6 Keep feeding the flowers in, saving the most delicate ones for last. Finish with the fluttery flowers.

7 Wrap the stems in floral tape and ribbon, and add a bow (page 162).

Cascading peach and pink

This lush bridal bouquet is an excellent example of a tone-on-tone arrangement. The various flowers are close in color, but each has a different shape. The magical combination creates a bouquet that is much more dramatic than one using only a single blossom. You could stop there, but why not add a few small surprises: a handful of salmon nasturtiums and sprays of pink abutilon and, for contrast, some metallic blue viburnum berries and coral arbutus flowers. If you can find a vintage blue embroidered ribbon like the one pictured here, it takes this splendid bouquet to another level.

ALTERNATE FLOWERS Replace the spirea with doublefile viburnum; the azalea with small rhododendron; the roses or other flowers with peonies, pink lilacs, or lilies.

11 FLORAL STEM WIRES, 18 GAUGE

RUBBER BANDS

FLORAL TAPE

1 YARD SALMON PINK RIBBON,
2 INCHES WIDE

STRAIGHT CORSAGE PINS

1 YARD BLUE RIBBON,
4 INCHES WIDE

5 SPIREA BRANCHES

4 SALMON-PINK AZALEA BRANCHES

8 METALLIC BLUE BUNCHES OF
VIBURNUM BERRIES

3 PINK-CORAL ARBUTUS FLOWERS

12 PEACH-PINK ROSES

6 PINK-AND-CREAM
FRINGED TULIPS

5 PEACH-PINK RANUNCULUS

16 PINK ABUTILON STEMS

8 SALMON NASTURTIUM STEMS

1 Trim any foliage from the lower part of the spirea branches. Trim the azalea branches in the same way, and layer the azalea branches on the spirea. These will form the base of the bouquet. See "How to Make a Cascading Bridal Bouquet," page 152.

2 Trim and wrap the tips of the viburnum and arbutus with floral wire.

3 Trim and remove the foliage from the roses, tulips, and ranunculus. Add some of the roses to the bouquet, followed by some of the tulips, interspersing throughout, and secure the bouquet with a rubber band when it gets difficult to hold. Add more roses, tulips, and the ranunculus, alternating the blossoms with the wired viburnum stems. Secure with a second rubber band.

4 Layer in the abutilon stems, making sure they are interspersed throughout the bouquet. Add the delicate nasturtium flowers one at a time. Finally, add the arbutus flowers, securing them with floral wire to the azalea stems so that they hang down off the bottom tip of the bouquet.

5 Wrap the stems in floral tape and ribbon as instructed on page 162, but instead of adding a looped bow, simply fold the blue ribbon in half and pin it at the fold to the base of the bouquet.

Bridal bouquet in shades of peach and yellow

spring, summer

Once you choose a basic color—in this case a yellowy peach—search for a variety of blossoms that fit this category. The challenge is to find flowers that take your basic color and run the scales with it, from taupe-yellow to butter, from gold to cream, from citrus to speckled.

It's particularly exciting when you find flowers that use the same color in a variety of ways. In this bouquet, for example, the veins of the striking variegated pitcher plant pick up the same burgundy that dots the freckled Vanda orchids and leaps from the heart of the tree peony.

ALTERNATE FLOWERS In fall, use dahlias as a focal flower, freesias or snapdragons as secondary flowers, and sweet autumn clematis for a vine. In winter, orchids are a good choice for a focal flower, as are amaryllis.

1 Start with the pitcher plant, trimming the stems but keeping them long so they can be clipped later. These will form the base of the bouquet.

2 Trim and place four branches of the Solomon's seal, making sure to keep the greenery behind the flowers.

3 Trim the flowers and add them to the bouquet, alternating the roundness of the peonies, carnations, and roses with the leggy petals of the lilies. Check the bouquet in a mirror as you proceed. Add more Solomon's seal, placing it toward the back of the bouquet. When the stems get too bulky to hold, wrap them with a rubber band.

4 Place the orchids strategically, making sure they fit between the roses and yellow peonies. Position the tree peony at the top of the arrangement so its full glory can be viewed by the bride.

5 Finish the bouquet with floral tape, ribbon, and a bow as instructed on page 162.

RUBBER BANDS

FLORAL TAPE

2 YARDS EACH PALE PINK, MAUVE, AND BURGUNDY RIBBON, 2 INCHES WIDE

STRAIGHT CORSAGE PINS

STAPLER AND STAPLES

---

8 VARIEGATED PITCHER PLANT STEMS

8 VARIEGATED SOLOMON'S SEAL STEMS

3 YELLOW PEONIES

6 PALE PINK CARNATIONS

5 'CARAMEL ANTIKE' GARDEN ROSES

5 CHAMPAGNE ROSES

3 YELLOW GLORIOSA LILIES

3 SPECKLED VANDA ORCHID STEMS

1 PEACH-BURGUNDY TREE PEONY

| # Lavender and white

"Summer afternoon; to me they have always been the two most beautiful words in the English language," wrote Henry James. This bouquet is as soft as a summer's day: a simple arrangement of pale lavender and white highlighted with summer greenery, all of which might be harvested from a backyard garden. What captures the heart is the corona of pale greenery around the small bouquet. The subtly striped ribbon, in pale lilac and white, echoes the floral tones.

ALTERNATE FLOWERS Replace the pincushion flowers with white roses or dahlias, the clematis with lavender and white sweet peas, and the greens with boxwood and Solomon's seal.

1 Begin by assembling the ferns, myrtle, and pittosporum as the base of the bouquet.

2 Layer in the longer clematis stems, both blue and white. Trim some of the clematis to shorter lengths, and alternate these with the pincushion flowers and sweet peas, making sure that the some of the sweet peas stand out from the bouquet like wisps. Add the stems of sweet autumn clematis to the greenery.

3 Fasten the bouquet with rubber bands. Finish the bouquet with floral tape, ribbon, and a bow as instructed on page 162.

RUBBER BANDS

FLORAL TAPE

2 YARDS LILAC-AND-WHITE STRIPED RIBBON, 2 INCHES WIDE

STRAIGHT CORSAGE PINS

STAPLER AND STAPLES

8 FERNS

8 MYRTLE STEMS

12 PITTOSPORUM STEMS

6 LAVENDER CLEMATIS STEMS

6 WHITE CLEMATIS STEMS

12 WHITE PINCUSHION FLOWERS

15 WHITE SWEET PEA STEMS

4 SWEET AUTUMN CLEMATIS STEMS

A trio of nosegays

Consider the charming nosegay, a small bouquet that, in earlier times, often delivered a message. Called "tussie-mussies" during the reign of Queen Victoria, these bouquets spoke the language of flowers: red roses symbolized romantic love and passion, pink roses implied a lesser affection, and yellow roses stood for friendship. Blue hyacinths meant constancy; purple asked for forgiveness. Bells of Ireland conveyed "good luck." You can make such small bouquets as graduation or get-well gifts, or for mothers of the bride and groom simply because they are so charming.

ALTERNATE FLOWERS Replace the ranunculus with roses or tulips; use iris instead of the orchids.

1 Build each bouquet from the inside out, starting with fifteen tightly gathered ranunculus. Trim and secure with a rubber band.

2 Each orchid has a "nose," or small stamen, that emerges from the flower. Pinch this off so the flower is entirely flat.

3 To extend the length of the orchid stems, poke a floral stem wire through the base of each orchid. Bend the wire in half so the ends meet, then wrap them, top to bottom, in floral tape (see photos at right).

4 Add five orchids to each bouquet so they surround the core of ranunculus and form the base of each bouquet. Secure them with a rubber band.

5 Finish the bouquets with floral tape, ribbon, and a bow as instructed on page 162.

RUBBER BANDS

15 FLORAL STEM WIRES, 20 GAUGE

FLORAL TAPE

1 YARD EACH RIBBON IN SHADES SIMILAR TO THE FLOWERS, 1/2 INCH WIDE

STRAIGHT CORSAGE PINS

STAPLER AND STAPLES

---

15 SOFT PEACH RANUNCULUS

15 PINK RANUNCULUS

15 COPPER RANUNCULUS

15 PHALAENOPSIS ORCHID STEMS, IN SHADES SIMILAR TO THE RANUNCULUS

HOW TO WRAP
WITH RIBBON AND
ADD A BOW

Wrap your bouquet in ribbons that are as beautiful as your flowers, and finish by adding a bow made out of loosely looped ribbon. This technique is much less fussy than a standard bow, and it couldn't be easier.

1 Wrap the stems of your bouquet in floral tape, leaving the bottom 2 inches of the stems uncovered.

2 Wind ribbon around the stems to hide the floral tape, starting at the bottom and working your way up to the flowers. Anchor the end of the ribbon with a straight corsage pin.

3 Select 2 yards of a ribbon that complements the color of the flowers. Make several loose loops, stapling the loops at their center. Cut a V into the ends of the ribbon.

4 Pin or wire the bow to the top of the stems. Feel free to add more ribbon and even combine multiple colors.

5 Place the entire bouquet in a container with 2 inches of water. It can be kept in water and refrigerated for 24 hours.

6 Remove the bouquet from the water right before the event, and trim off the bottom 2 inches of stems.

Three chartreuse and brilliant pink bridesmaid bouquets

Hot pink tree peonies practically shout, "Pick me, pick me!" They are the perfect focal flower for a trio of pink and green bridesmaids' bouquets. But the real key to the success of these bouquets is the more plebian 'Queen Red Lime' zinnia. This one blossom, with its multiple shades of green and pink, ties all the contrasting elements together. The long, tubular blossoms of lime green nicotiana and the bright green ivy balanced by dark green vinca and chocolate geranium leaves make a combination that will pop against bright or pale pink bridesmaids' dresses or light up black ones. Add a pink ribbon and start the procession.

ALTERNATE FLOWERS Replace the peonies with hot pink roses, ranunculus, or dahlias. Use bells of Ireland instead of the nicotiana. Chartreuse variegated ivy might be a good substitute for the *Stephanandra incisa*; common ivy would work just as well.

1 You don't have to use the exact number and type of flower in each bouquet. Each arrangement can be a little different and therefore unique. However, these instructions are for three matching bouquets.

2 Build each bouquet from the inside out, making sure three tree peonies are located toward the center.

3 Take five each of the two types of zinnias, plus five each of the roses, carnations, and nicotiana stems, and alternate them to balance the colors, breaking up the combination with the addition of foliage: seven chocolate geranium leaves, five coleus, and seven *Stephanandra incisa*. Fasten each bouquet with a rubber band.

4 Carefully intersperse two lilies and four vinca stems into the flowers to add contrast.

5 Finish each bouquet with floral tape, ribbon, and a bow as instructed on page 162.

RUBBER BANDS

FLORAL TAPE

3 YARDS BRIGHT PINK RIBBON, 2 INCHES WIDE

STRAIGHT CORSAGE PINS

STAPLER AND STAPLES

---

9 HOT PINK TREE PEONIES

15 'QUEEN RED LIME' ZINNIAS

15 GREEN 'ENVY' ZINNIAS

15 'YVES PIAGET' ROSES

15 PINK 'HURRICANE' CARNATIONS

15 LIME GREEN NICOTIANA STEMS

21 CHOCOLATE GERANIUM LEAVES

15 BURGUNDY AND GREEN COLEUS

21 *STEPHANANDRA INCISA* VINES, OR ANY IVY

6 *WHITE ACIDANTHERA* LILIES

12 VINCA STEMS

Autumn dahlias

In the early fall, when there is a nip in the air, it's exciting to watch the trees begin to turn from green to burgundy and gold. Inspired by that time of year, this bouquet is a celebration of dahlias, accompanied by spidery lilies and a collection of pale carnations. Vines are abundant at this time of year, and this bouquet uses the flowers of the cup-and-saucer vine with abandon.

ALTERNATE FLOWERS Replace the dahlias with roses, the carnations with zinnias. Use passion flower or sweet autumn clematis vines instead of the cup-and-saucer vine.

RUBBER BANDS

FLORAL TAPE

2 YARDS PALE PINK RIBBON, 2 INCHES WIDE

STRAIGHT CORSAGE PINS

STAPLER AND STAPLES

6 REDDISH BROWN WINGED EUONYMUS BRANCHES

5 RED-AND-WHITE DAHLIAS

5 PEACH DAHLIAS

7 BUFF CARNATIONS

5 WHITE CARNATIONS

6 PINK SNOWBERRY STEMS

6 PINK *NERINE* LILIES

3 *CYRTANTHUS* LILIES

3 BEIGE ANTHURIUM FLOWERS

10 CUP-AND-SAUCER VINES

9 'TWINKLE' ONCIDIUM ORCHID STEMS

1 Start with a base of euonymus branches, and alternately add the dahlias and carnations. As the width of the base increases, secure the stems with a rubber band and continue to build.

2 Feed in the snowberry stems, followed by the lilies. Place the anthurium flowers at the back and outside of the bouquet so they create a "collar." Add the cup-and-saucer vines, interspersing them among the other flowers.

3 Finish with the stems of the tiny white orchids, allowing them to flutter above the top and sides of the bouquet.

4 Finish the bouquet with floral tape, ribbon, and a bow as instructed on page 162.

Champagne boutonniere

These boutonnieres are fashioned from putumayo carnations, which have a sophisticated champagne tone with hints of pale green, beige, and peach. Just the thing to match a bride's ivory gown.

ALTERNATE FLOWERS Often it's best to use a flower for the boutonniere that is featured in the bride's bouquet.

1 Trim the carnation stems to about 2 inches. Pass a floral stem wire through the base of each flower, bending it in half (similar to the orchid-wiring technique; see top photo on page 161). Trim the olive stems to the same length.

2 For each boutonniere, wrap a carnation and an olive stem together with floral tape.

3 Wind a ribbon around the stems of each boutonniere, from bottom to top. Secure the end of the ribbon with a hot glue gun. Refrigerate the boutonnieres in a plastic container for up to 24 hours before your event to keep them fresh. Use corsage pins to attach the boutonnieres.

5 FLORAL STEM WIRES, 20 GAUGE

FLORAL TAPE

1 YARD PALE PEACH SILK RIBBON, ¼ INCH WIDE, CUT INTO 5 EQUAL PIECES

GLUE GUN

5 STRAIGHT CORSAGE PINS

5 PUTUMAYO CARNATIONS

5 RUSSIAN OLIVE STEMS

Compotes

A compote is a raised bowl. It lends itself well to lush table arrangements because the footed base lifts the flowers toward eye level without blocking a guest's view. The wide bowl allows for fullness, letting the flowers relax into their natural postures, sometimes spilling onto the table. The wide opening also means you can build a complex arrangement that appears to float horizontally. Vines wrapped around the pedestal add a touch of whimsy.

Our grandmothers used these footed bowls for fruit and nuts, but they are actually the perfect vessel for holding flowers. On dining tables, branches can reach out horizontally so even small compotes can make a large impact. Because the bowls are wide, compotes welcome bodacious flowers on short stems that drape over the edge of the bowl. In fact, the best compote arrangements let flowers and vines swoop down to and even touch the tabletop.

Ceramic, silver-plated, glass, pottery, and pewter footed bowls can be found in department and housewares stores as well as at flea markets and floral supply houses. Choose the material based on the style of your arrangement and where you plan to put it. Terra-cotta fits a rustic outdoor setting, burnished silver glows at a formal occasion, and porcelain is so versatile it can work well in either.

HOW TO BUILD A BASIC COMPOTE ARRANGEMENT

Use these steps as a general guideline to help you build most of the compotes in this chapter.

1 Attach a pin frog to the center of the compote with floral putty. Fill three-quarters full with water. Often, it's good to place your compote on a lazy Susan so you can turn the arrangement and view it from every angle.

2 Remove the lower leaves from branches. Clip so they are one and a half to two times the height of the compote. Cut an X in the bottom of each stem. If the compote will be against a wall, one branch should stand upright, and the others should be positioned to the right or left to form the base layer. If the compote will be on a dining table and will be viewed from both sides, the branches should be horizontal, arching outward over the compote.

3 If you have more than one type of branch, trim and clip the other branches, and intersperse them among or on top of the first branches.

4 Trim and add the foliage, filling in between the branches.

5 Build the arrangement from the outside in, trimming and adding flowers, starting with the largest blooms.

6 A variety of stems should be trimmed short so they sink into the compote or hang over the edge. Remember, this is a horizontal arrangement so you don't want much height.

7 Trim and add the vines, wrapping some through the flowers and winding others down and around the foot of the compote.

8 Trim and add the focal flowers. If this is a table arrangement, position them on both sides so they face diners. They should either hang over the compote or stand out from the arrangement.

9 Wrap more vines into and around the compote.

10 Step back and observe the compote. Look for spots that would benefit from a few more flowers.

Fragrant white

White flowers bring a dramatic touch to evening events. The blossoms glow as if illuminated from the inside. Night is the time when lilacs and jasmine release their most potent scents, so this arrangement will delight the nose as well as the eye.

ALTERNATE FLOWERS Replace the orchids with peonies, the bay laurel with mock orange (*Philadelphus*), the almond branches with unripe pears, the freesias with snapdragons, the narcissus with carnations, and the jasmine with clematis. Any white flowers would work in this arrangement.

1 Anchor a pin frog at the bottom of the compote with floral putty. Fill three-quarters full with water.

2 Trim the almond branches, and cut an X in the bottom of each. Arrange in the compote as an inverted triangle with some of the fruits hanging over the edge of the compote. This will be the base layer (see page 174). Trim the bay laurel branches, and cut an X in the bottom of each. Position in the compote next to the almond branches.

3 Trim the geraniums and intersperse between the other branches. Trim the lilacs and position horizontally. Trim the spearmint and freesias, and add to the arrangement, alternating white and green. Trim and add the hyacinth in groups of two or three.

4 Trim and add the gardenias, making sure they appear on both sides of the compote. Trim the sweet peas, and intersperse them between the other flowers. Trim the jasmine into 4-inch pieces, and position in the arrangement so some rest above the edge of the compote and others slip in next to the lilacs.

5 Place each orchid stem in a plastic tube filled with water so they are properly hydrated in the compote. Position one orchid at the top of the arrangement, and two tucked in over the opposite edges of the compote.

6 Stand back and look at the arrangement. Place the narcissus in groups of three and five wherever you see an opening. Trim and add the pepperberries. Finish by wrapping the *Clematis montana* vine around the base of the compote and using the akebia vine as a halo for the entire arrangement.

GLASS COMPOTE, MEDIUM

PIN FROG

FLORAL PUTTY

3 PLASTIC WATER TUBES
(SEE PAGE 47)

---

3 FRUITED ALMOND BRANCHES

3 BAY LAUREL BRANCHES

7 PEPPERMINT-SCENTED
GERANIUM STEMS

5 WHITE LILAC BRANCHES

7 SPEARMINT STEMS

12 WHITE FREESIAS

10 WHITE HYACINTH, SOME STILL
IN GREEN BUD FORM

12 WHITE GARDENIAS

16 WHITE SWEET PEA STEMS

6 JASMINE VINES

3 WHITE CATTLEYA ORCHID STEMS

12 WHITE-AND-ORANGE NARCISSUS

3 GREEN PEPPERBERRY SPRIGS

3 *CLEMATIS MONTANA* VINES

3 AKEBIA VINES

luminous yellow

RANUNCULUS

VARIEGATED
BOX-LEAF AZARA

ALMOND
BRANCHES

CYMBIDIUM
ORCHID

TULIP

PARROT TULIP

SPIREA BRANCHES

ABUTILON

MEYER LEMON

Luminous yellow

"Nature's first green is gold," wrote poet Robert Frost about the fresh unfurling of spring. How glorious, after a long winter, to behold fields of yellow mustard, bold crocuses, and cheerful daffodils. This arrangement embraces a softer palette but one that reflects all the joyful emotions of spring. Green and white are natural companions for yellow, with a favorite purple hellebore added for a cheeky accent.

ALTERNATE FLOWERS Replace the ranunculus with roses. Use flowering apricot or hawthorn branches instead of the spirea, pear branches instead of the lemon branches, and narcissus instead of the tulips.

WHITE CERAMIC COMPOTE, LARGE

PIN FROG, LARGE

FLORAL PUTTY

---

15 TO 20 SPIREA BRANCHES

7 VARIEGATED BOX-LEAF AZARA BRANCHES

5 FRUITED ALMOND BRANCHES

5 MEYER LEMON BRANCHES WITH FRUIT

10 YELLOW RANUNCULUS

8 YELLOW-GREEN RANUNCULUS

4 YELLOW-BURGUNDY PICOTEE RANUNCULUS

7 YELLOW PARROT TULIPS

7 FRINGED YELLOW TULIPS

3 YELLOW CYMBIDIUM ORCHID STEMS

8 WHITE ABUTILON BRANCHES

5 MAROON-MAUVE HELLEBORES

1 Secure a large frog at the bottom of the compote with floral putty. Fill three-quarters full with water.

2 Trim the spirea branches, and cut an X in the bottom of each. To make a base layer (see page 174), arrange all but four of the branches vertically in the compote, with others spilling to either side. Trim the azara and almond branches, and cut an X in the bottom of each. Place next to the spirea. Remove the leaves from the lemon branches, cut an X in the bottom of each, and position the branches so some of the fruits overhang the edge of the compote.

3 Trim the ranunculus, cutting some stems short so the flowers hug the center of the arrangement. Add to the compote in groups of two or three.

4 Trim the tulips, leaving them tall so they rise above the ranunculus. Position them between the spirea and the almond branches.

5 Trim the orchids and the abutilon. Both should be anchored on either side of the compote to make the arrangement more horizontal. Some of the abutilon can even graze the tabletop.

6 Place the hellebores in the top and sides of the arrangement. Finish by adding the remaining spirea branches to either side, extending the horizontal quality of the compote.

TULIP

PARROT TULIP

HYACINTH

PURPLE CHERVIL

CHECKERED LILY

Smoky mauve

RANUNCULUS

GRAPE HYACINTH

HELLEBORE

NASTURTIUM
VINES

Smoky mauve

Is the color mauve purple, smoky gray, pink, lavender, or all of the above? It's such a sophisticated color, reminiscent of kings and gilded-age glamour. This arrangement finds inspiration in an extraordinary Parrot tulip called 'Secret'. It's ruffled and deeply serrated, and looks like a wild purple cabbage. The tulip stands out in this arrangement, where it is complemented by purple-and-white-striped ranunculus and bold lavender hyacinths.

ALTERNATE FLOWERS Replace the tulips with purple orchids. Use anemones instead of the ranunculus.

1 Anchor a pin frog to the bottom of the compote with floral putty. Fill three-quarters full with water. Trim the hellebores, and position them around the edge of the compote.

2 Trim the Parrot tulips, keeping them 10 to 12 inches long, and arrange them so they arch over the compote.

3 Cut the standard tulips slightly shorter. Intersperse them among the Parrot tulips and the hellebores. Trim both types of hyacinth. Place each in a different section of the arrangement.

4 Trim the ranunculus. Add to the compote, alternating small and large, striped and solid flowers. Trim the lilies and intersperse them throughout the arrangement.

5 Trim the chervil stems. These act like fern fronds. Drape them from either side of the arrangement.

6 Trim the nasturtium vines. Anchor them and wrap them through the arrangement, letting some swing down below the edge of the compote.

GRAY COMPOTE, MEDIUM

PIN FROG

FLORAL PUTTY

---

5 PURPLE-MAUVE HELLEBORES

12 'SECRET' PARROT TULIPS

5 STANDARD PURPLE TULIPS

5 STANDARD PURPLE AND WHITE-EDGED TULIPS

3 PLUM HYACINTHS

5 GREEN GRAPE HYACINTHS

7 GRAPE RANUNCULUS

7 PURPLE-STRIPED RANUNCULUS

8 CHECKERED LILIES

5 PURPLE CHERVIL STEMS

2 NASTURTIUM VINES, FOLIAGE ONLY

Orange zest

Nothing packs more punch than an orange poppy that seems to explode with color. Poppies are just as exotic in their bud stage, when their bulbous heads dance on sun-seeking stems. This compote marries those paper-thin petals with sturdy ranunculus and pretty nasturtiums. Start with the majestic *Fritillaria imperialis*, a regal flower that, in this arrangement, acknowledges its own majesty by appearing to take a bow. This small compote lets the flowers dominate and spread out as if embracing the room.

ALTERNATE FLOWERS It is hard to find orange flowers with the same impact as the ones in this arrangement, but try coral peonies, peach tulips, and roses.

1 Anchor a pin frog at the bottom of the compote with floral putty. Fill three-quarters full with water.

2 Trim the fritillaria, and position at the center and on the right and left. Place one so it hangs over the edge of the compote.

3 Trim the ranunculus and poppies to varying heights, and place them alternately in the compote. Allow the poppy buds to hover over the rest of the flowers.

4 Add the nasturtiums, letting some hang over the edge of the compote and positioning others to float above. Trim the raspberry tips, and place them so they hang over the edge of the compote.

PEWTER COMPOTE, SMALL

PIN FROG

FLORAL PUTTY

---

3 *FRITILLARIA IMPERIALIS*

10 ORANGE RANUNCULUS

20 ORANGE ICELAND POPPIES

8 ORANGE NASTURTIUM, INCLUDING LEAVES

5 RASPBERRY LEAF TIPS

Modern rose

Let's not forget the rose, the queen of the garden. "My love is like a red, red rose," wrote poet Robert Burns, and, indeed, that sentiment still stands. Many people see red roses as the definition of romance.

This red rose compote is a great example of a tone-on-tone arrangement. A deep-red garden rose called 'Tess' is the focal flower, followed by a deep fuchsia 'Darcey' rose and a Nobbio carnation called 'Black Heart', which combines both tones. A spray rose called 'Black Baccara' combines with the rusty leaves of the copper beech to complete an arrangement that looks like red velvet. The eye moves from one shade of red to another. Clustering two or more of each flower avoids a polka-dot effect. The aim is to achieve subtle waves of color that draw the eye.

ALTERNATE FLOWERS You can achieve a similar look using a variety of red peonies in the spring and dahlias in the fall. What you are aiming for is tones of red and a variety of flower shapes. Use clematis foliage in place of the akebia, rhododendron tips instead of the azalea.

1 Anchor a pin frog to the bottom of the compote with floral putty. Fill three-quarters full with water.

2 Trim the akebia vines. Fasten each into the frog, then wrap it around the foot of the compote.

3 Trim the copper beech branches, and cut an X in the bottom of each. Anchor them into the frog so one is in the center and the other two are on either side.

SILVER COMPOTE, MEDIUM

PIN FROG

FLORAL PUTTY

2 OR 3 AKEBIA VINES

3 COPPER BEECH BRANCHES

12 'TESS' GARDEN ROSES

15 'DARCEY' GARDEN ROSES

10 NOBBIO 'BLACK HEART' CARNATIONS

6 'BLACK BACCARA' SPRAY ROSES

6 AZALEA BRANCH TIPS

CONTINUED

Modern rose, continued ‖ 4 Trim four or five 'Tess' and 'Darcey' roses so they hang over the lip of the compote, letting them relax into their natural posture. As you build the arrangement, keep the subsequent rose stems longer. Place the remaining roses in groups of two or three. They should undulate, leading the eye into the bouquet.

5 Trim the carnations and the 'Black Baccara' roses. Add between the other roses to enhance the color pairing. Don't pack the blossoms too tightly, or the arrangement will be too rigid.

6 Trim and add azalea tips next to the roses so their green color contrasts with the redness of the roses.

USE ROSE PETALS

Loose rose petals artfully arranged at the base of your compote can enhance the impact of an arrangement. Or, on a long table, you can sprinkle them the entire length. Better still, if you have leftover roses that have lost their stems, remove the sepal that fastens the petals, and place the resulting whorl upside down beneath your arrangement. It's an easy bit of theater that always enchants.

Celebrating with flowers

Some occasions deserve more than a little fanfare. Why not surprise your guests—and yourself—with an unusual arrangement that enhances a happy moment? Sometimes these gestures can be small, but they can make a big impact through repetition—like harvesting a magnificent crop of dahlias and placing them in individual vases down a long dining table. Sometimes they can be grand, such as pulling out all the stops on an outdoor urn arrangement that will welcome people to an anniversary celebration.

In traditional Indian weddings, the simple marigold is used to make a glamorous impression. Its spicy fragrance fills the room, as petals are strewn in the bride's path and long chains of the orange flower decorate doorways. Stringing flowers for special occasions is a technique that you can also use with sweet carnations to decorate a wedding couple's chairs, with roses to wrap a chuppah, or with greens to fashion a crown for a birthday girl.

Decorating chandeliers with flowers adds an impressive touch to a special dinner party. Suspended above a summer dining table and woven with ferns and orchids, it helps set the dimensions of an outdoor room.

How can you plan for these dramatic moments? When you survey a location, make note of an entranceway or a lovely, but unadorned, corner. Look up. Is there a way to suspend flowering garlands from the ceiling or attach them to church pews? When you are using large numbers of flowers with abandon, remember your budget. Better to employ less expensive blossoms, like marigolds or carnations, and scavenge for large but simple items like tree branches that can be simply arranged in a large urns.

RANUNCULUS

CLEMATIS MONTANA

SPIREA

FREESIA

FRINGE TREE
BRANCHES

Elegant white

FOXGLOVE

GARDENIA

Elegant white

"White is not a mere absence of color; it is a shining and affirmative thing," wrote novelist and philosopher G. K. Chesterton. "God . . . never paints so gorgeously . . . as when He paints in white." I agree. White can stand alone beautifully. There is nothing more sophisticated than an all-white arrangement, especially one that combines various flower shapes and heights, from open and blowsy to regal and tall.

Most narrow-necked vases in this collection contain a single variety of white flower. It's amazing how such simplicity results in such a sophisticated table setting. The flowers are all spring bloomers, but any varieties of whites in any season will achieve the same effect.

Your goal is to create a range of floral impressions—from a single, elegant ranunculus upright in a small vase to a cascade of tightly packed spirea in another, taller vase. Each flower reflects its own nature: the snaking vines of *Clematis montana* crawl across the table; the hyacinth bends in a great arch. Not only is each flower different, but each is different in the way it sits in the vase.

ALTERNATE FLOWERS In summer, use 'Casa Blanca' lilies, campanula, clematis, and cosmos. In fall, chrysanthemum, clematis, dahlia, and Japanese anemone. In winter, amaryllis, *Eucaris* lily, and paperwhite narcissus.

8 NARROW-NECKED GLASS VASES
IN VARYING SIZES

---

3 PALE GREEN HELLEBORES

3 WHITE FOXGLOVES

4 WHITE RANUNCULUS

5 WHITE FRINGED TULIPS

6 WHITE SPIREA BRANCHES

3 WHITE GARDENIAS

2 WHITE *MICHELIA*
MAGNOLIA BRANCHES

2 WHITE KOUSA
DOGWOOD BRANCHES

2 WHITE *CLEMATIS*
MONTANA BRANCHES

5 WHITE FREESIAS

5 FRINGE TREE BRANCHES

1 Fill each vase three-quarters full with water.

2 Trim the branches and flowers to a variety of heights. The key is to vary the height of the flowers as well as the vases, matching tall flowers with the taller vases and shorter, rounder flowers with more rounded vases.

3 Experiment with placement. You can alternate one tall and two short vases, gather three in a group, or march them right down the center in the order of size.

PURPLE PARROT TULIP

FRITILLARIA
UVA-VULPIS

RANUNCULUS

PEACH PARROT TULIP

CHECKERED LILLY

WHITE *FRITILLARIA
PERSICA*

HELLEBORE

ORANGE PARROT TULIP

Dutch masters

PURPLE *FRITILLARIA PERSICA*

CHRYSANTHEMUM

Dutch masters

This style of flower arranging is much emulated but often misunderstood. Most Dutch floral paintings from the seventeenth century incorporate every flower in the lexicon, in every shade, from every season—the opposite of tone-on-tone arrangements. The arrangement here uses spring flowers—these always seem the most Dutch—and a multitude of them. Emphasis is placed on two contrasting colors—orange and purple, with multiple shades of each. A sprinkling of white blossoms adds a painterly gleam, further highlighting the contrast.

ALTERNATE FLOWERS Use peonies or dahlias instead of the tulips, hawthorn or apple boughs instead of the rose canes, carnations instead of the ranunculus, foxglove or snapdragon instead of the fritillaria.

1 This vase is tall enough so it doesn't need an anchor. Fill three-quarters full with water.

2 Trim the rose canes and position them in the vase to establish a base layer (page 37). Because this is such a dramatic arrangement, leave the canes long. Some should extend 2 feet above the vase.

3 Trim the viburnum branches, and cut an X in the bottom of each. Alternate them with the rose canes.

4 Trim the tulips. Some should be cut short, about 5 inches, and set deep into the vase. Other varieties, especially the purple and peach Parrots, should be long, about 10 inches, and allowed to arch over the vase. Intersperse the tulips in the arrangement.

5 Trim the ranunculus. Like the tulips, some should be cut short, others left longer. Add to the vase in groups of three.

6 Because the chrysanthemums are large flowers, they should be trimmed and placed individually. Do not let them stand out from the other flowers, or they will be too dominant. Trim the checkered lilies and intersperse throughout.

7 Trim all varieties of fritillaria. Add individually to the arrangement. Let some rise high, above the vase, and anchor others so they dip low, even touching the table.

8 Trim and anchor hellebores so they hang over the edge of the vase.

TALL GLASS VASE, MEDIUM

---

12 WHITE MINIATURE ROSE CANES

5 GREEN VIBURNUM BRANCHES

5 PURPLE PARROT TULIPS

5 PEACH PARROT TULIPS

5 ORANGE PARROT TULIPS

5 WHITE PEONY TULIPS WITH RED EDGING

5 PURPLE FRINGED TULIPS

6 GREEN PICOTEE RANUNCULUS WITH PLUM EDGES

6 ORANGE-PEACH RANUNCULUS

5 PLUM-TONED CHRYSANTHEMUMS

10 CHECKERED LILIES

6 PURPLE *FRITILLARIA PERSICA*

6 WHITE *FRITILLARIA PERSICA*

6 *FRITILLARIA UVA-VULPIS*

5 GREEN HELLEBORES

Hair garland

Flower crowns are popular with today's brides, and they have always been adorable on young bridesmaids. Make these garlands for a sweet sixteen party or any midsummer fete. You can use several feet of paddle wire to fashion the beginning halo, wrapping it in floral tape before attaching the greenery, or you can use pipe cleaners, which are even easier. Once you gather the requisite greens and the flowers or buds you want to attach, the assembly is easy.

ALTERNATE FLOWERS Replace *Pieris japonica* with boxwood, swamp maple with variegated arborvitae, lily buds with rose buds, and use ivy as your vine.

1 Attach the pipe cleaners end to end. Twist to form a circle that fits the head of the wearer.

2 Lay the *Pieris japonica* tips along the pipe cleaner circle. Attach the first tip to the crown with a piece of stem wire. Place the next stem on top of the first, and fasten with stem wire. Continue until the entire wreath is covered.

3 Space the maple pods evenly around the garland and wire securely. Do the same with the lily buds. Wrap the entire garland in wire vine to cover the floral wire. The vine is clingy and does not require any fastener.

4 Spray the garland with water and refrigerate in a plastic bag for up to two days until ready to use.

3 GREEN PIPE CLEANERS

25 FLORAL STEM WIRES, 20 GAUGE

15 *PIERIS JAPONICA* TIPS

5 VARIEGATED SWAMP MAPLE PODS

5 BLUSH *NERINE* LILY BUDS

3 CREEPING WIRE VINES

Fern chandelier

A playful addition to any party, this chandelier is decorated with
plumosa and leatherleaf ferns, inexpensive varieties that can remain out
of water for a long time—up to two days—which makes them suitable for
this kind of arrangement. Each orchid stem can be set into an individual
tube of water, but these flowers will also last for a day or two without
drinking. This circular brass chandelier was discovered at a flea market,
but since you cover it in ferns, any round structure might do, even two
24- or 30-inch round wire wreath forms wired together for greater depth.
This wreath was suspended over the outdoor table using a metal pole
fastened to two adjoining buildings, but depending on your location,
you may have to use other methods.

ALTERNATE FLOWERS Any kind of sturdy fern will do: umbrella fern,
for example. This also looks nice without flowers.

1 Hang your chandelier at a height at which you can work on it. Depending
on the size and shape of the chandelier, you may need to attach the ferns
with floral stem wire. Wrap the wire around the fern stems and then attach
to the chandelier. Or if the openings on the chandelier are wide enough,
you can just weave the ferns through.

2 Fill the plastic tubes with water, and place each orchid stem in a separate
tube. Hide the tubes beneath the fern foliage so they do not show. Wrap
floral stem wire around each tube and attach to chandelier. The orchids
should stand out against the solid green background.

3 Move or hoist your chandelier to its final location or height and attach
it securely. You don't want it falling down on guests! Mist the arrangement
in advance of your event.

CIRCULAR CHANDELIER

12 TO 62 FLORAL STEM WIRES,
20 TO 24 GAUGE

12 PLASTIC WATER TUBES
(SEE PAGE 47)

20 PLUMOSA FERN BRANCHES

30 LEATHERLEAF FERN BRANCHES

12 GREEN MINIATURE
PHALAENOPSIS ORCHID STEMS

Celebrating with flowers   211

Fruit garland

The definition of abundance, fruited garlands are like a cornucopia spread out and come to life. They are quite easy to assemble. Yes, you have to wire the foliage but, once you've done that, the colorful fruits are simple to arrange. Guests can admire the garland's beauty as well as feast on its bounty. You can choose any number of vines—just make sure they are thornless. Thimbleberries, common to California and the Pacific Northwest, are a form of raspberry that boasts a downy maplelike leaf that is both pretty and perfect for this creation. The amount of fruit you use depends on the length of your table. This recipe covers a 6-foot table.

ALTERNATE FLOWERS thornless blackberry or grapevine.

1 Measure the table you want to cover. Trim the branch tips. Lay one tip halfway on top of another, and wrap them with wire. Continue overlapping and wiring the branch tips, periodically adding the hawthorn flower buds. The foliage of both should hide the wire. Stop when you have reached the desired length.

2 Position the garland along the edge of the table. The final garland will be almost 1 foot wide. You don't need to anchor the garland, since the fruit will hold it down. However, if you are using an inexpensive wooden table, you can hold the garland in place with a few thumbtacks.

3 Starting with the larger fruits, like the pears, arrange them so the fruits sit on the leaves at the front and back of the garland, anchoring it in place. Add the smaller fruits and nuts, alternating reds and yellows with greens and golds.

FLORAL PADDLE WIRE,
20 TO 24 GAUGE

THUMBTACKS (OPTIONAL)

20 THIMBLEBERRY BRANCH TIPS

7 HAWTHORN FLOWER BUDS

7 PEARS

24 GREEN PLUMS

30 QUEEN ANNE CHERRIES

15 APRICOTS

25 GREEN UNHULLED ALMONDS

Marigold curtain

In Europe during the sixteenth century, the poor would place a bouquet of yellow flowers before a statue of the Virgin Mary to signify their devotion to the church. Known as "Mary's gold," this colorful offering soon came to be called the "marigold."

Today, many gardeners see marigolds as a simple garden flower, something planted to keep insects from tomato plants. In various cultures, the blossoms are a great signifier. In Mexico, they decorate family graves on the Day of the Dead. In India, long strings of marigolds are draped as offerings at Hindu temples. Orange marigolds, so important at Indian weddings, are a symbol of creation and regeneration, and are thought to bring good luck to the newlyweds. The scent is as appealing as the color: the marigolds fill the air with a pungent, peppery fragrance that spells anticipation.

A marigold curtain is easy enough to assemble, though it requires time, patience, and a way with an upholstery needle or a Hawaiian lei needle, which can be ordered online. This recipe should make five lengths of marigolds, each about eight feet long, sufficient to hang over a door. Note that for marigolds of this quantity, you will have to order them from a flower market or find a local grower.

ALTERNATE FLOWERS Substitute other inexpensive flowers, such as carnations or chrysanthemums.

1 Make sure the marigolds are well hydrated. Keep them refrigerated in buckets overnight.

2 Thread the needle with a length of monofilament. Knot and tie a safety pin at the opposite end so the first flower has something to rest against. Clip off the marigold stems, leaving just the heads, and begin stringing by passing the needle through the center of each flower from base to top. When the garland reaches 8 feet, tie a secure double knot and attach another safety pin. Leave the remaining 2 feet of monofilament for hanging the garland. Repeat to make the remaining four garlands.

CONTINUED

5 LENGTHS OF 20-POUND-TEST MONOFILIMENT FISHING LINE, EACH 10 FEET LONG

3- TO 8-INCH HAWAIIAN LEI NEEDLE

10 SAFETY PINS

LARGE PLASTIC BAG (OPTIONAL)

HAMMER

5 NAILS, WITH HEADS, EACH 2 INCHES LONG

300 TO 400 ORANGE MARIGOLDS

3 If not using the garlands immediately, place them in a large plastic bag and refrigerate to keep the flowers fresh. Marigolds are sturdy and will last for three or four days in the refrigerator.

4 Before your event, hammer the nails along the top of the doorway. Never use thumbtacks; these are weighty arrangements. Wrap the monofilament of each garland several times around a nail and tie a knot.

5 Once they are hung, the garlands' freshness depends on the weather. If they are in the shade or the weather is mild, they will certainly last a day or two. If they are in the sun and it is very hot, they may wilt sooner. You can help keep the curtain fresh by spraying it periodically with water.

Dahlias down the table

A blossom at its peak of bloom is a wonder to behold. Take this chorus of dahlias gathered on a single day in September. The perfect blooms in shades of pale or peachy pink are placed in different vases in tones of gray and light pink, adding some geometry to the mix but never detracting from the flowers.

When you have flowers as dramatic as these dahlias, let them do the work. Pick a variety of vases of similar heights, trim each blossom to the proper length, and start playing with placement. Notice that all the vases here have skinny necks—the one requirement for a display of one or a few blossoms. It's best to choose a limited palette. This pairing of pink and gray is classic, but you might try yellows and oranges against gray, or fuchsia against navy blue.

1 Fill each vase three-quarters full with water.

2 Remove the foliage from the flowers. Clip the dahlias so the flowers sit snugly in the vases. All should be a similar height. Some vases will hold one dramatic bloom. Others may hold two or three smaller flowers.

24 NARROW-NECKED VASES OF
SIMILAR SIZES AND HEIGHTS

24 TO 36 DAHLIAS IN SIMILAR
SHADES AND VARIOUS SIZES

Giant outdoor urn arrangement

This abundant urn could hold center stage at a wedding or other celebration. It's laden with branches of tree-ripened apples, olives, and clematis that look as if they were picked fresh from the farm. Add a generous serving of carnations and a fancy-pants flower like store-bought phalaenopsis orchids, and you have showtime. Color provides continuity in this arrangement, with blossoms transitioning from pink to mauve. But it's the juxtaposition of plain and fancy that makes the arrangement special.

ALTERNATE FLOWERS Replace the apples with pears or other fruited branches. Use dahlias instead of the carnations, and pink lilies instead of the orchids.

1 Insert a waterproof container, such as a plastic bucket, into the urn. Attach a large flower frog to the base of the bucket with floral putty. Fill the bucket three-quarters full with water. If there is still space around the bucket, fill with balled-up newspaper.

2 Trim the apple branches, and cut an X in bottom of each. Arrange the branches to form a base layer (page 37) so they drape over the urn and almost touch the table.

3 Trim both types of olive branches, and cut an X in the bottom of each. Add to the urn, with some forming a background fan and others dipping to either side and dangling outside the urn.

4 Trim the orchids. Concentrate these dramatic blossoms in a group toward the front of the arrangement. Trim the carnations. Add fifteen carnations to the left side of the urn. You need to group them together so they don't get lost in the arrangement. Place the remaining five carnations individually throughout the arrangement.

5 Trim the lilac clematis vines and add one at a time. They should act as floaters, rising above the other flowers. Trim the sweet autumn clematis vines. Wrap over and around the arrangement.

FOOTED, CAST IRON URN, LARGE

WATERPROOF CONTAINER, LARGE

PIN FROG, LARGE

FLORAL PUTTY

NEWSPAPER, IF NEEDED

---

6 APPLE BRANCHES WITH GREEN FRUITS

5 FRUITED OLIVE BRANCHES

3 RUSSIAN OLIVE BRANCHES

6 MAUVE ORCHID STEMS

20 VIOLET-BEIGE CARNATIONS

12 LILAC CLEMATIS VINES

5 SWEET AUTUMN CLEMATIS VINES

Succulent and tillandsia wreath

This is a long-lasting wreath that is easy to build in any season (but do not hang it outdoors in freezing temperatures). Lichen and moss set the gray-green palette, which is reinforced by a variety of succulents and the tillandsias. Tillandsias are known as "air plants" because they can grow without soil. They are often found suspended in trees. Hobby shops sell metal wreath forms in multiple sizes that can be decorated with all manner of greenery. It's best to pick ingredients that have some shelf life: dried hydrangea blossoms, lichen-covered branches (like the ones used here), or eucalyptus leaves. All will last for three months or longer. You can find plenty of materials right in your own backyard.

ALTERNATE FLOWERS Chinese lantern flowers, eucalyptus berries and leaves, grapevines.

1 Lay overlapping branch tips on the wreath form and wrap with floral wire. The branches should spike outward from the form.

2 Stuff the moss between the branch tips and the wreath form. This creates a gray-green base and conceals the wire.

3 Poke a length of wire through the base of each succulent and wire it to the form. Do the same with the tillandsias. They should be positioned asymmetrically around the wreath. Make a wire loop measured to fit the door or wall on which you will hang the wreath. To keep the succulents and tillandsias perky, occasionally spray the wreath with water.

20-INCH CIRCULAR METAL
WREATH FORM

FLORAL PADDLE WIRE,
20 TO 24 GAUGE

30 LICHEN-COVERED
BRANCH TIPS

REINDEER MOSS

10 ASSORTED SUCCULENTS

10 ASSORTED TILLANDSIAS

Using local flowers in arrangements whenever possible is better for the environment and results in more vibrant, natural, long-lasting arrangements. Of course, availability differs depending on where you live and the time of year. Whether you shop a flower or farmers' market or gather from your own backyard, you'll find more and better-quality blossoms if you make your choices based on seasonality.

Depending on where you live, some flowers may bloom slightly earlier or later than listed on the following page. There are some flowers that are available year-round in flower markets. Those will appear on more than one list.

Seasonal flower guide

SPRING

Allium
Anemone
Apple, peach, plum,
    crabapple, and
    cherry blossoms
Calla lily
Checkered lily
Daffodil
Dogwood
Euphorbia
Forsythia
Foxglove
Freesia
Fritillaria
Gardenia
Grape hyacinth
Hellebore
Hyacinth
Iris
Gloriosa lily
Lilac
Lily—Asiatic, oriental, hybrids
Magnolia
Mock orange (*Philadelphus*)
Narcissus
Orchid
Peony
Pitcher plant
Pussy willow
Ranunculus
Rose
Tulip
Viburnum
Wisteria

SUMMER

Abutilon
Agapanthus
Allium
Amaranthus
Anemone
Arbutus
Batchelor button
Calla lily
Campanula
Carnation
Castor flower
Clematis
Cockscomb
Cosmos
Daisy
Delphinium
Dianthus
Foxglove
Freesia
Gardenia
Gentian
Gladiola
Globe thistle
Heuchera
Hydrangea
Jasmine
Lady's mantle
Larkspur
Lily—Asiatic, oriental, hybrids
Lisianthus
Love in a puff
Marigold
Nasturtium
Nicotiana
Orchid
Phlox
Pincushion flower
Poppy
Ranunculus
Rose
Russian olive
Sweet pea
Sweet William
Veronica
Zinnia

FALL

Amaranthus
Aster
Calla lily
Carnation
Chinaberry
Chocolate lace flower
Chrysanthemum
Clematis
Coxcomb
Dahlia
Eucalyptus
Hydrangea
Lily—Asiatic, oriental, hybrids
Love in a puff
Orchid
Rose
Snowberry
Sunflower
Zinnia

WINTER

Amaryllis
Calla lily
Lily—Asiatic, oriental, hybrids
Narcissus
Orchid
Roses

Ariella Chezar

In her twenty years in business, Ariella Chezar has created designs for hundreds of weddings and events, including Christmas at the White House. She has taught her popular Flower Workshops, upon which this book is based, throughout the United States and in the Netherlands.

Ariella trained with two talented New England floral designers, Pamela Hardcastle and Barbara Bockbrader. She started her career selling holiday wreaths on a New York City street corner, later working for floral designer Robert Isabel.

In 1998, Ariella moved to San Francisco, where she began designing in a more open and abundant style, reacting to the floral bounty of the West Coast. While there, she published *Flowers for the Table*, published by Chronicle Books, a guide to choosing seasonal flowers.

Ariella returned to the Berkshires in 2003, where she lives with her husband and two children. Together, they purchased Zonneveld Farm in 2013.

As a designer, Ariella has been profiled in numerous magazines, including *Martha Stewart Weddings*, *Oprah*, *In Style Weddings*, *Sunset Weddings*, *Garden Design*, *Elegant Bride*, *Town & Country*, *House and Garden*, *Victoria*, and *Sunset* magazine.

Julie Michaels

A writer and editor based in western Massachusetts, Julie has been an editor at the *Boston Globe* and *New England Monthly* magazine. She has written for the *Globe*, the *Wall Street Journal*, and the *New York Times*, as well as numerous magazines. A principal in Spence & Sanders Communications, Julie tends a large vegetable and flower garden in West Stockbridge, Massachusetts.

About the Authors

Acknowledgments

This book exists because of Leslie Jonath. I have so much gratitude for her persistence, her unwavering belief in the project, and her ability to keep me on track.

Much additional thanks to:

Erin Kunkel for making my work look so beautiful. With your ease, confidence, and grace, you make magic time and again.

Julie Michaels for your friendship, your patience, and your beautiful way with words. I have loved working on this book with you.

Glenn Jenkins for your lay-down magic, for always knowing what was needed and for transforming a perfectly fine setup into so much more.

Editor Lisa Regul, who first saw the potential of this project and guided it to fruition. Copyeditor Judith Dunham for your deep attention to detail.

Emma Campion for your gorgeous design—a happy combination of freedom and support. Margaux Keres for your vision.

Garden editor Julie Chai for your insight and Elise Cannon for getting us started.

Sarah Silvey, adopted sister and constant support. Your friendship is such a gift.

Max Gill for your friendship, always, and for the marvelous tidbits from your magical garden.

Tess, for your patient marigold stringing, and ever-present support. Stephanie Hughes for your hard work and sweet company. Fallon Anderson for your glorious roses. Jenya, my dear friend.

Kaye and Richard Heafey for creating one of my favorite places on earth, Chalk Hill Clematis, and for allowing me to work on its beautiful grounds.

Tom and Suky Werman for allowing me to photograph at Stonover Farm.

Chris, for standing by me through everything, and for building me a flower farm.

Simone and Tarame for being there, always, and Howard for your unwavering support.

Index

Published in the United States by Ten Speed Press,
an imprint of the Crown Publishing Group, a division
of Penguin Random House LLC, New York.
www.crownpublishing.com
www.tenspeed.com

Ten Speed Press and the Ten Speed Press
colophon are registered trademarks of
Penguin Random House LLC.

Library of Congress Cataloging-in-Publication Data is
on file with the publisher.

Hardcover ISBN: 978-1-60774-765-9
eBook ISBN: 978-1-60774-766-6

Printed in China

Design by Emma Campion
and Margaux Keres

10 9 8 7 6 5 4 3 2 1

First Edition